D0451018

enjoy japan

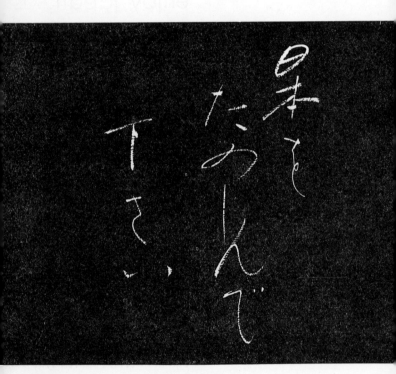

日本をたのしんで下さい。

illustrated by Sanae Yamazaki

walt sheldon

enjoy japan

A PERSONAL AND HIGHLY UNOFFICIAL GUIDE

charles e. tuttle company

RUTLAND, VERMONT : TOKYO, JAPAN

Representatives

For Continental Europe: BOXERBOOKS, INC., Zurich
For the British Isles: PRENTICE-HALL INTERNATIONAL, INC., London
For Australasia: BOOK WISE (AUSTRALIA) PTY. LTD.
104-108 Sussex Street, Sydney 2000
For Canada: HURTIG PUBLISHERS, Edmonton

Published in Japan by the
Charles E. Tuttle Company, Inc.
of Rutland, Vermont & Tokyo, Japan
with editorial offices at
Suido 1-chome, 2-6, Bunkyo-ku, Tokyo

Library of Congress
Catalog Card No. 60–15609

International Standard Book No. 0-8048-0170-3

First edition, 1961
Nineteenth printing, 1976

0200-000119-4615
Manufactured in Japan

table of contents

PART TWO

places

foreword

THE KEY TO ENJOYMENT

The dew has left my eyes. After nearly a decade in Japan I am no longer intrigued by pastel lanterns, bamboo parasols, flowery kimono, geisha hair-dos, bows and smiles—and I am bored, bored, bored with cherry blossoms.

Yet here I am, enjoying Japan.

I am, with many other foreigners, irritated by the gross public manners of the Japanese, so different from their exquisite politeness in the home. I am terrified by the suicidal city traffic.

Still, I'm happy here.

My sense of international good will leaves me several times a day when gardeners, carpenters, plumbers, and other tradesmen blithely fail to show up for appointments; when tailors and dressmakers cheerfully produce highly original creations different in every particular from what was ordered; and when, in the night, inebriated Japanese gentlemen use my garden for a urinal.

I stare, astounded, at policemen who in their turn stare, unmoved, at unlawful acts performed beneath their very noses. I listen in amazement as at a single rally one group shouts: "Yankee, go home!" and another group raises a howl because the

Yankees are doing just that and letting a few employees go in the process.

However, I'm here—liking it.

The overdone interpretation of sex offends me. At Minsky's a stripper may often, by a sort of art, be provocative—in Japan, the bumps and grinds most often look just plain dirty. Bad taste is rampant. A popular lipstick, widely advertised on television, bears the candid trademark: "Sexy Pink." Vocalists imitate popular U.S. and European records note for note, inflection for inflection, and pass the performance off as their own. Pimps and gangsters hang around street corners in aloha shirts, tight pants, duck-tail haircuts, and hard white faces. Their consorts use too much lipstick and wiggle into tight sweaters lumped by obviously phony "PX-chichi," or falsies.

I am infuriated by the red tape of bureaucrats which, by comparison, makes the stodgiest Occidental government procedure look like leaping free enterprise. My sense of logic is shaken by such methods as that of the electric company, which charges you a higher rate per kilowatt *if you use more.*

But, with freedom of choice, here I am.

Have I complained enough? You see, I wanted to get that part of it over with. And I wanted you to know that I am no recently arrived foreigner still dazzled by Japan's undeniable surface charm. For it's not entirely the surface charm I want to deal with; it's what I've found beneath, that which has kept me here this long and will, I hope, keep me here a few more decades.

The fact is, I'm in love with Japan.

But—with all these complaints—why?

Ask any in man in love, "Why?" You'll never get a clear answer. There is so much that goes to make up a feeling of deep affection, so much that must be sensed rather than delineated on graphs or put into words. It's my hope that some of it will come through in this book, perhaps as an overtone, and that you will begin to see why I, and a few score others I know, truly love Japan. And that you yourself will learn, at the very least, to enjoy the place.

This book came about because of a series of radio programs entitled "Enjoy Japan" which I have been doing for some years for the Far East Network, the broadcasting outlet of the U.S. forces stationed here. It follows the pattern of the radio program, which is designed to interpret Japan for the benefit of Americans living in closed communities which sometimes tend to be out of touch with the local scene. It is an official policy of the U.S. Forces here to encourage mingling and understanding between military Americans and their Japanese hosts. This is a most laudable policy, and you can be sure that any standoffishness or feeling of superiority on the part of Americans springs from the few individuals who would probably have a hard time fitting in anywhere, even in their own home towns. Yet even for those with the desire to know more, introductions, orientations, and interpretations are needed. The program "Enjoy Japan" has perhaps contributed here in a small way.

I am not an expert on Japan. I am neither sociologist nor linguist, but merely a more than ordinarily curious American with some journalistic and literary training. Any competent reporter could have assembled the material I've found and many, I'm sure, could have done it more quickly and thoroughly. My only claim to anything unique is that in the process of investigating Japan I fell in love with her—which, I admit, sounds like the plot of a bad movie.

And so, from this curious standpoint, I present this book. It will have two lines of development, running in counterpoint. There will be factual information, as there might be in a guide book. There will also be the highly personal observations and reactions of an American who came here after seeing much of the rest of the world, decided to stay, lost the dew from his eyes, and still found that he had made a happy and rewarding union.

Dozo . . . *irashaii-mase.*

Enter . . . and Enjoy Japan.

W. S.
Tokyo, 1961

PART ONE

people

chapter one

the geisha

It's almost always the first question a visitor asks when he gets off the boat or plane:

"What about the geisha? What about them—*really?*"

Understandable. The subject is fascinating, as are the ladies themselves. And though many foreigners have visited or lived in Japan in recent years, the rumors and false notions about the geisha persist. There are several reasons for this. One lies in the various definitions, many inaccurate and many only partly accurate, given to the word "geisha." Another is that geisha do not ordinarily welcome foreigners as customers; and still another is that geisha entertainment comes high—it's one of the most expensive attractions Japan has to offer.

Well, what about them, then? What about them, really?

We had better first know what we mean by "geisha," whose first syllable is pronounced to rhyme with "gay" and not with "glee." The word is used most loosely and erroneously. In the Western world "geisha" is a generic term embracing everything from a Japanese folk dancer to a downright prostitute. But the true geisha—the first-class geisha—is something quite different. There's nothing like her anywhere in the world.

geisha—past and present Geisha, we say. "Gei" means talent . . . "sha" is a person. Thus the geisha, etymologically speaking, is a talented person. In Kyoto, the heart of geishadom, she is usually called "geiko" which means, roughly, a talented young lady.

Scholars find the first mention of the word "geisha" in A.D. 1762, which would seem to indicate that they're a comparatively recent phenomenon; but female entertainers of much the same type are mentioned in Japanese chronicles as early as A.D. 1100. There were also, in feudal times, a group of nomad female performers called *asobime,* or "play girls," who wandered from town to town and sought engagements. Another early name for lady entertainers was *shirabyoshi.* There were even young women of noble blood who played, sang, and danced at court, and served as companions to the men gathered there. Probably their companionship did not go too far or become too intimate. At one period, however, we find some female dancers called *odoriko* whose conduct, the dusty records briefly and tantalizingly show, caused the government to issue an ordinance for the "maintenance of morals."

In modern Japan dozens of types of female entertainers and

companions are called, loosely, "geisha." At the very top of the
scale we have the true geisha who are, basically, entertainers—
nothing more. They live in special geisha districts in all the big
cities. They're apprenticed to the profession at an early age and
are seldom, as romantic writers would have you believe, taken
from poor families as children and sold into a sort of white slavery.
The average young girl is as thrilled and honored to enter geisha
training as she might be to become a stage personality or a movie
star.

Training is begun at various ages, sometimes as early as seven,
sometimes as late as sixteen. A large percentage of the girls come
from families associated with geisha houses—teahouse and restaurant people, for instance. Geishadom, like show business, is
a kind of world of its own. Not a few apprentices are the daughters
of geisha who have been married, or have at least entered into
an amiable common-law arrangement.

the appren- The young geisha-to-be works very hard. She
tice geisha studies with acknowledged masters in singing,
dancing, acting, and the playing of various
Japanese instruments. She lives in the *nishu,* or geisha quarters
(a sort of exotic sorority house), and in these surroundings undoubtedly picks up professional tips from all the full-fledged geisha. Her art requires more than mere stage perfomance; a geisha
has to know how to keep the conversation lively with a visiting
male dolt; she has to know how to put a party at ease and keep
it going with various games. And, like Pagliacci, she has to mask
her own emotions if she is troubled.

Apprentice geisha are known as *maiko* in Kyoto, and as *oshyaku*
in the Tokyo area. They wear their kimono, obi, and hair in a
different fashion from the graduate geisha and, in addition to
their studies, they act as greeters, serving girls, and sometimes

performers in the geisha and tea houses. To see a lovely young maiko strolling through one of the narrow streets of a geisha section is one of Japan's most arresting sights. Youth adds to the beauty of these geisha-to-be—but oddly enough a geisha need not be of stunning physical appearance to achieve success. Personality and talent are considered more important.

Maiko, when they begin their careers, are housed, clothed, and fed by the geisha house which later offers their services to the customers. Careful accounts are kept of this investment. It's quite expensive to develop a geisha, paying for her schooling and keep, and later, when she makes her debut, providing her with an entirely new set of kimono. Geisha and maiko kimono cost a great deal more than the ordinary kind and the young ladies, who are much in the public eye, must have dozens of changes on hand. All in all, this large investment binds most young geisha to their parent houses until it is paid off and a profit realized.

private life of a geisha   Geisha are hired out by the hour or evening. Their presence, plus the surroundings of the tea-house or restaurant, gives the average Japanese gentleman a chance to relax in the atmosphere of Old Japan—to get away for a while from the hum of generators, the honking of taxis, and perhaps even from the scolding of a sharp-tongued wife. At a geisha party meals and refreshments are served. The geisha converse with the customers, tell jokes, play games, dance and sing. Foreigners often find a genuine geisha party somewhat dull, because much of the enjoyment depends on fluency in the language and an inherent knowledge of Japanese culture and folkways.

After the party the geisha leave and the gentlemen are free to wrap up the evening at a cabaret or other place of entertainment. The true geisha does not ordinarily spend the night with the customer, any more than a chorine in the Western world consistently hires herself out to every talent scout or pickle merchant who comes along. She may, of course, have her special patrons or gentleman friends. She may, on occasion, be in a financial bind and unable to resist taking the relatively easy way out of it. Doubtless some geisha have interesting nymphomaniacal tendencies. This sort of thing happens in Western-world show business and café society too, but we don't automatically think of actresses or show girls as prostitutes.

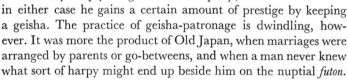

If a geisha enjoys a patron, he is usually a man of means who may be in love with her or who may simply delight in her company; in either case he gains a certain amount of prestige by keeping a geisha. The practice of geisha-patronage is dwindling, however. It was more the product of Old Japan, when marriages were arranged by parents or go-betweens, and when a man never knew what sort of harpy might end up beside him on the nuptial *futon*.

The patron pays most of the geisha's bills, which can reach a staggering total, and often he may live with her in a house or cottage which he visits when time permits. Geisha are usually faithful to their patrons and only in romantic novels do they have poor but handsome boy friends on the side.

pillow geisha Now, at the bottom of the scale we find in Japan thousands of untalented women who *pretend* to be geisha, and who are referred to as such in more-or-less tongue-in-cheek fashion. These girls can be hired at hotels in cities and popular resorts and in the cheaper restaurants and tea houses. They're often called *makura-geisha*—*makura* meaning pillow. They will join a stag party in a hotel room and go through the motions of singing, dancing, or playing the samisen, but their performance is usually third rate and their real contribution comes privately, later in the evening.

Unfortunately these "pillow geisha," and other party girls who offer themselves in varying degrees, have given rise to many of the false impressions about geisha held by foreigners.

The truth is difficult for a visitor to discover. It's not even easy for a Westerner to conclude an assignation with a pillow geisha, should he find himself in the mood for some red-blooded, he-man entertainment. It requires a certain finesse, and without fluency in the language the whole affair is likely to become complicated.

You may ask, at a resort inn, for a couple of geisha to be sent to the party in your room. You'll be charged for them later on your bill, and you'll be charged plenty. For this you may get no more than a few songs, a couple of foolish party games, and someone to sit beside you and keep filling your glass. If, however, the young lady is amenable, you might be able to make private arrangements for later. At extra cost. On the whole, it's not worth it. Not afterward, in the cold light of morning, with a hangover.

geisha and foreigners
You will also, as a foreigner, find it almost impossible to plan a *true* geisha party on your own. The tea houses don't like to entertain Westerners —they feel that it always leads to too much misunderstanding and complication. The great bulk of their business is done with known customers, who are billed several weeks later. The transaction is always polite and discreet. The best chance to witness a genuine geisha party is to have a Japanese friend throw one and include you as a guest. It might be well to know that anyone who essays this will spend a young fortune.

On the whole, the visitor to Japan will find himself regarding the geisha from afar . . . glimpsing them, perhaps, as they scuttle from a house to a waiting covered rickshaw (the last few rickshaws left in Japan are mostly for carrying geisha to their appointments), or seeing them on the stage, in movies, or on television. Many of them make extra money by such appearances. You may see a geisha proudly accompanying her patron at a night club. He has bought her time; he may take her anywhere, short of the boudoir. And when you see such a geisha you will be struck by her elusive, subtle expression . . . at once innocent and wicked, at once bold and coy. There will be the trained grace of a dancer in her every movement; utter femininity in her vanity, and the apotheosis of womanhood in her apparent breathless interest in her companion.

And so, even when you know all the facts, the geisha remains exotic, mysterious, tantalizing, desirable.

She is woman—only more so.

chapter two

the gods

We are at once profane and pious, we Occidentals. I've asked hundreds of Japanese: "What are the first things foreigners want to know about your country?"

The first thing, they reply, is always the geisha.

The second is religion.

There are two principal religions in Japan and these are Buddhism and Shinto. We call them religions for lack of a more accurate word. Neither is quite a religion in the sense that Christianity, Judaism, and Islam are, though Buddhism comes closest to the definition. When regarding Shinto, however, as we shall presently in more detail, it's important to put aside all pre-formed notions of what a religion ought to be, for only in that way will you begin to understand it. And you must also keep in mind that while Buddhism is the predominant religion in Japan and a great many people profess it, many of them also practice a certain amount of Shinto. Pleasantly confusing? Well, this is Japan for you.

Christianity, too, is a religion of Japan, but without a wide membership. In 1930 it claimed about 250,000 adherents; in 1947 the count was 350,000 and differing reports at this writing put it at about 400,000. Usually these statistics are based on church memberships only, so there may be more who actually consider themselves Christians. Or, if there are enough backsliders still on the rolls, there may be fewer.

buddhism　More than half the country's population may be counted as Buddhist, and probably there are a great many more who haven't been counted or registered. Buddhism in Japan, however, is something uniquely Japanese, even though it was originally imported from the mainland of Asia. Indeed, you will often hear it said, and rather proudly too, that "Buddha receives more devotion in Japan than in the land of his birth—India."

The official date of the arrival of Buddhism in the Japanese islands is A.D. 552. A king of Korea, by name Kudara needed help in one of his civil wars and sent presents to the Emperor Kimmei of Japan. Among these gifts were Buddhist images and *sutra,* the Buddhist scriptures. Before long, priests, nuns, and temple architects followed. Kimmei was intrigued by the new religion and tried to promote it in Japan, at first without too much success. It wasn't until nearly half a century later that Prince Shotoku managed to popularize it.

Buddhism in Japan, for the first two centuries, remained quite Chinese in character. Then it split itself into two main sects, Tendai and Shingon, both of which had adapted their precepts more fittingly to the Japanese way of life. At this point, as a matter of fact, many of the Shinto deities were incorporated into Japanese Buddhism and declared to be other manifestations of Buddha himself—Bodhisattvas. (This is really no more remarkable than an early Christian practice in the United States which emphasized, for the benefit of various Indian tribes, those saints' days that fell on the dates of the tribes' accustomed pagan festivals.)

Today there are about sixty different Buddhist sects in Japan, and some of these are divided into sub-sects. Their beliefs range from the austere precepts of Zen, which is currently drawing interest in the U.S., to the more amiable theology of the widespread Shin and Nichiren sects.

Generally speaking, Buddhists in Japan revere and worship Buddha. He is both God and Savior. They call him "Hotoke-sama," so don't be puzzled if a Japanese friend doesn't understand the word "Buddha" if you speak it.

Buddha—to recall the story briefly—was a noble young prince of India who one day broke away from his family and wandered as a beggar for six years, looking for truth. One night he went to sleep under a tree and when he awoke everything had seemed to come to him in a flash. This tree is now one of the most important symbols of Buddhism everywhere. And what Buddha learned is summed up, though hardly explained, in these tenets:

(1) The middle path is best. Moderation. Neither extreme asceticism nor excessive devotion to earthly pleasure will bring true contentment.

(2) There are four great truths to be considered:
   (a) To exist is to suffer at times. There's simply no way out of it. (b) The cause of all suffering is the desire to gratify the senses. (c) There is a possibility of escaping this dependence on the senses and becoming detached and passionless in feeling. (d) The way to do this is through

something called the Eightfold Way, which involves Right Views, Right Resolve, Right Speech, Right Action, and so on.

(3) The goal of all this is a kind of unassailable serenity called Nirvana, which of course very few ever attain.

Modern Buddhist sects differ mainly in what they regard as the better methods of attaining this ideal state. Some of the sects come very close to Christian ideas of Heaven and Hell; others are more concerned with reincarnation and may teach that if you growl too much about things in this life you may come up as a dog in the next.

Buddhism, compared to other major religions of the world today, is a rather gentle, rather passive creed. Most sects are not militantly interested in making converts. Respect for immediate ancestors is apt to be an important part of a Buddhist's feeling, and most Japanese Buddhists will keep a little shrine in the home, bearing a picture or some other memento of the deceased father or grandfather of the house, so that small daily offerings may be placed before it. This is purely a symbolic gesture; most typical is a bowl of rice, left there a day or so, after which it may be retrieved and eaten by anyone who cares for cold rice. A Buddhist who receives a present may put it on the shrine for a while before he uses it. This once happened to a bottle of whisky I gave a Buddhist friend of mine.

And there is another incident I have always thought of as characteristically Buddhist. Once I discovered that a neighbor of mine was busily sweeping out my garden, which adjoined his, every morning. I told him that this part was *our* garden and that, really, we'd get around to sweeping it ourselves one of these days. He smiled and said that it was his Buddhist feeling to do this—to do a few little things every day for someone else. It made him feel good, he said. I believed him, and still do. But I think his secret is also known by certain right-neighborly rural folk in the United States.

This is Japanese Buddhism, then, but one doesn't gain even a glimpse into the Japanese character without considering Shintoism, too. I have said that Shintoism is not, in the Western sense, a religion. Perhaps it's more accurate to say it's a cult, though that doesn't quite describe it either. We'll use "religion" for lack of a better word, but please be aware of the qualifications as they unfold.

shinto First, Shinto is purely Japanese. Second, it embraces both nature and ancestor worship. The chief deity is Amaterasu-O-Mikami, the Sun Goddess, who figures largely in Japan's creation legend. But there are scores of other gods: the early chronicles mention some eight million! In Shinto almost anyone or any *thing* can be a sort of god. The Japanese word for god, or spirit, is *kami,* but it doesn't necessarily mean a personified deity. It can also be the spirit or essence of a person, an animal, a tree, a rock, a mountain—even an idea. In this respect Shinto is remarkably like the nature worship of some of the American Indians.

Amaterasu, the principal figure in the Shinto pantheon, is considered the ancestress of the present emperor who, by the way, comes from the longest unbroken line of rulers in the world. She is also responsible for the big double-yoked gateway you see at the entrance to all Shinto shrines: the inescapable feature of the Japanese landscape called the *torii.*

According to the legend, Amaterasu became angry at her ne'er-do-well brother one day and shut herself in a cave. Since she *was* the sun, the world was plunged into darkness. The other gods tried repeated ruses to get her out and finally hit upon the idea of placing a crowing cock at the entrance to the cave. When

Amaterasu heard the sound, she thought it was morning and emerged. The world was light again. And the torii, or gateway? This is the perch on which the crowing cock was placed.

the shinto shrines The shrines are anywhere and everywhere in Japan. There are huge ones like the Meiji Shrine in Tokyo or the Grand Shrine at Ise, and there are small ones in back yards. You find them on lonely mountaintops, in the courtyards of industrial plants, or even on the roofs of department stores. They may be dedicated to one of the legendary gods; they may honor a famous individual. They may express the spirit of an animal—the sect of the fox shrine is very popular—or simply that of a mountain, rock, or tree.

A visit to a Shinto shrine is felt by most Japanese to be purifying. There is nearly always a little font near the entrance where you briefly wash your lips before entering. Shinto priests do a great deal of ceremonial bathing. The average Japanese, as a matter of fact, has an almost religious regard for his frequent ordinary bath.

At the shrine itself you go before the altar, usually in a house of some kind, clap your hands twice or thrice, bow your head a moment and pray for purification or protection against evil. You may wish for something you want, or you may wish for someone else's good fortune. There's usually a small receptacle where you can toss a small amount of money. Ten yen will do; more, if the spirit moves you. The receptacle is barred on top to foil collection-plate filchers.

There's no real system of theology or ethics in Shinto, though some recent sects have been trying to develop and promote these things. Shintoists are quite tolerant and you, as a foreigner, won't at all offend anyone if you decide you'd like to offer a prayer or make a wish yourself at one of the shrines. On the contrary, the onlookers will be amused and pleased.

Many devout Buddhists pray at a Shinto shrine now and then. So do a great number of Japanese Christians, rather to the dismay of their teachers, I fear. It's because Shinto has a national, patriotic, and perhaps tribal feeling for the Japanese. This could be compared to the patriotic emotions felt by Americans at the Lincoln memorial or by Britons in Westminster Abbey.

support of shrines and temples You will have wondered by now who supports all these temples and shrines in Japan. (Buddhist places of worship are *tera*—temples, and Shinto places are *jinja*—shrines. You can tell them apart by the torii, or gateway, in front of all shrines.) The Buddhist temples are usually supported by the faithful themselves, though some are kept by the government as national treasures. The Shinto shrines are largely supported by the government, but quite often by the neighborhood in which they stand, and now and then by individuals.

There is also a loose "Popular Shinto" consisting of an almost infinite number of deities locally or individually chosen and frequently enshrined in private homes. Shrine shops, where all the paraphernalia may be bought, are prosperous in Japan. In Tokyo a huge cluster of these establishments may be seen in the neighborhood of Asak'sa, where there are also a number of important Buddhist temples. There, at the huge temple of Kannon, the goddess of mercy, it's customary to purchase incense sticks before entering, place them in a little sand-filled kiosk near the entrance before lighting them, and then scoop smoke on your neck and shoulders for purification.

now and zen A great many Americans who come to Japan for the first time will want to know in particular about Zen, perhaps the best known, in the Western world, of the Buddhist sects. Zen is an austere philosophy which gets all sorts of interpretations in the West, especially by the restless cry-babies who call themselves the Beat Generation. Zen itself has broken into three sub-sects: Rinzai, Obaku, and Soto. In general Zen teaches that Buddha's ideas are much too profound for mere words and must be felt through strict discipline and silent meditation. The historical founder of Zen was an Indian monk Bodhidharma, who, in the sixth century A.D. sat for nine years doing

nothing but staring at a blank wall. The search for the elusive, wordless truth in Zen leads to some remarkable situations. A pupil, after some hours of meditation, may look up at the master and say something like: "What is the true meaning of nothingness?" The master will then whack him over the head with a bamboo rod. Perhaps it is this sort of thing that strikes the Beatnik followers of Zen as Nothingville at its most. Or perhaps bamboo rods on the head are what they really need.

the religious outlook in japan The Japanese, then, are both amiable and tolerant in their religions, and in saying this we dismiss the temporary violent interpretations of Shinto that were used to incite some of the population to disagreeable behavior in World War II. The West, with its history of inquisitions and witch hunts, is not entirely guiltless on this score.

On the whole, today's Japanese are not readily upset by religious discussions or arguments which forcefully present a point of view different from theirs. What I mean to say is that it is probably safer to bring up the subject of religion at a Japanese sakè session than it is at a Western cocktail party.

The Japanese have adopted the Christian festival of Christmas as a purely secular holiday of their own. Crowds throng the downtown streets, store windows glitter with displays, and smiling, sloe-eyed Santa Clauses stalk the sidewalks. Not a bar or cabaret closes its doors. Christmas is one vast Saturnalia, but there's no blasphemous intent behind this because the average Japanese is simply not aware of the average Westerner's emotional attachment to his religion.

A favorite Tokyo story has two drunks staggering down the street at Christmas time, passing a church, and seeing the open doors and lights within. One nudges the other. "Whaddaye know?" he says. "They celebrate Christmas in churches, too!"

And the great national holidays of Japan are celebrated often enough in shrines or temples by worshipers who have had a cup or two too much. In Japanese religious feeling there is not the sense of prohibition or sin that one finds in the West. Yet there is unmistakable piety, reverence, and a groping for moralistic behavior. If you can grasp this attitude, you will be on your way to understanding the religious outlook of the Japanese.

chapter three

seven lucky gods—and a saint

In Japan the faces of the Seven Gods of Good Fortune (like the eyes of Texas elsewhere) are upon you. All the livelong day. You will see them in souvenir shops, temples, homes, and on the desks of foreign residents. I have ridden in taxis where one or more hung on the dashboard. Since they're so ubiquitous, you'll want to get acquainted with them.

They were once Buddhist gods, and they emigrated from China, but that was quite a while ago and now they've gone native.

They've also lost much of their religious significance, although you can still find a few shrines or temples dedicated to them.

seven together The Seven Gods of Good Fortune are called in Japanese: *Shichifuku-jin*. That looks formidable until you break it down. *Shichi* is seven, *fuku* is happy, *jin* is person or being, or in this case "god."

The seven are nearly always displayed together and their names, if you don't speak Japanese, are a little hard to remember, but not their characters. Each one has a definite face, figure, and personality. If you know the clues you can identify each of them any time.

Let's list them first:

1. EBISU: God of fishermen and tradesmen.
2. DAIKOKU: God of wealth; patron saint of farmers.
3. BENTEN: A lady god. Art, music, and eloquence.
4. BISHAMON: The god of war.
5. FUKUROKUJU. A wise god.
6. JUROJIN. God of longevity.
7. HOTEI. A happy and generous beggar god.

Together they make a decorative set for any mantelpiece, and they're a popular and highly authentic souvenir of Japan. You can get a clay set of the Seven Lucky Gods for a few cents, a beautifully carved wooden set for several dollars, or, if you can afford it, you can get them in jade or other precious material for several hundreds of dollars.

Often you'll find them shown aboard a sailing ship. This is known as *Takara-bune,* or the Treasure Ship. It comes into harbor every New Year's Eve, and if you put a picture of the ship under your pillow you'll have lucky dreams.

But now, let's form a reception line and meet our seven lucky spirits one by one.

ebisu   You'll always know him by the fishing rod he carries
         and the large, oval, pinkish fish under his arm. The fish
is *tai,* or sea bream, a delicious food fish with a delicate white
meat not eaten often enough in Europe or America. The Japanese consider it a symbol of good luck and congratulation, and
are apt to serve it at such affairs as promotion parties.

Ebisu's ancestry is somewhat mixed. Some believe he never
was a Buddhist god but the third child of Prince Isanagi and
Princess Izanami, who once stirred the sea with their spears and
made the Japanese islands. Others believe he's an offspring of
Daikoku, one of the other six gods.

At any rate, Ebisu will handle all matters pertaining to fishing,
food, and fair dealing. So if you see a stout little fellow with a
goatee, fishing rod, and sea bream under his arm—that's Ebisu.

daikoku   Daikoku is wealthy, and you can see this by the huge
           sack filled with precious things that he carries. You
also find him standing on rice bales, and if you look closely
you'll notice a rat or two nibbling at the bales. That's because
Daikoku is so prosperous he can afford to have a few rats free-
loading all the time. The rats also act as his messengers.

You'll notice he carries an ornate mallet in one hand. This is
a magic mallet, which functions rather like Aladdin's lamp.
Strike it, and you get anything you want.

Daikoku stands for wealth and plenty, and is the patron god
of farmers. As far as I know he pays no capital-gains tax.

benten   She's the only lady in our group and her longer name
          is Benzaiten. She's thought to be derived from one
Sarasvati, an Indian angel, and she always carries a *biwa*—a Japanese lute that looks like a combined mandolin, guitar, and
muskmelon. She can play the thing, too. Now and then, in ad-

dition to the lute, she totes a white snake around with her. You may ask your psychiatrist what this is supposed to symbolize.

bishamon   Standing sharply erect at the right hand of the lady, here's the god of war—Bishamon, sometimes Bishamonten. He's clad in armor from head to toe and carries a spear. That fuzzy stuff under his armor looks like wolfskin. He's a pretty fierce character altogether, but not entirely warlike. Look closer. That's a small pagoda in his other hand, and it means that he's not only a warrior but a missionary of virtue, for the pagoda is a place of worship and a reminder of religious obligations. Bishamon has a messenger, too—the centipede. When he says to his messenger: "Shake a leg!" he means it.

fukurokuju   You can't mistake him. His dolichocephalic head looks as though someone had grabbed on top and pulled. He's more or less the elder statesman of the group and can also be recognized by the scroll or symbol of learning he carries. He was originally a Chinese hermit and is said to have a secondary M.O.S. as God of the South Polar Star. The stork is his messenger, but as far as I know, this particular stork doesn't bring babies. As we said—he's a wise god.

jurojin   Old man; long, white beard. Kind of bent over and leaning on a staff. He stands for long life and is usually accompanied by one of the Japanese animal symbols for long life: the crane, the stag, or the tortoise. The deer is his special messenger.

hotei   Hotei is quite fat and always looks jolly. Sometimes he's shown in a gay pose with his arms extended and one foot lifted in the air, as though in a dance step. He has a huge stomach and that's supposed to indicate his inner wealth and largeness of soul. (Don't laugh—the soul may be in the stomach, at that.) Hotei is as bald as a thousand-year-old duck egg and keeps all his worldly possessions in a sack which he carries around with him.

I know Hotei comes from China, because I've met him there. In that country he's called Hotai, which rhymes with bow tie. The word means "cloth bag." Some scholars link him with an actual historical character, a beggar priest who lived in China in the tenth century A.D.

Before Hotei goes you have to drop a coin in that little beggar's bowl he carries. You might have bad luck if you don't.

Well, there you have the Seven Lucky Gods, and I think if you buy a set of their images you'll get to know and enjoy them. But these gods, with their rather worldly concern for such things as wealth and war, are more or less for the grown-ups. There's also a special deity for the kiddies, and we'll meet him right now.

jizo-sama   If you drive through the Japanese countryside you'll frequently come across roadside statues of a figure known as Jizo-sama. Chances are, you'll mistake them for representations of Buddha, for Jizo-sama looks rather like him. He has the same bland face and long ear lobes, and as he squats in place he holds one hand with the fingers extended in the graceful Buddhist sign of contemplation.

As a matter of fact there is some confusion, even among scholars, about the true identity of Jizo-sama. Some will tell you that he's another manifestation of Buddha, and Lafcadio Hearn states that he was once a human being who had learned the trick of living simultaneously on six different planes of existence. (Sounds like a science-fiction story.) Today he retains six different forms of divinity. As Jizo, he's the patron of children; as Koya, of pregnant women; as Hana-kake, of travelers; as Ago-nashi, of those with the toothache. And so on, down the line.

Now, when you see a roadside statue of Jizo you'll always notice a pile of stones in front of it. There's a story behind this. It seems that the nether world is separated from our mortal stamping grounds by a river called Sai-no-kawara, which corresponds to our River Styx in Western mythology. Souls have to cross this river but Sai-no-kawara, unlike the Styx, has no ferry service.

A gruesome hag and merciless she-devil named Shozuka-no-baba stands on the banks of this dark stream. She doesn't bother adults much, but when the souls of dead children come along, the first thing she does is to steal their clothes. Then she shows the children a huge pile of stones and tells them they have to build towers along the banks, and if they make the towers high enough they'll be able to reach Paradise.

This, as you've probably already guessed, is a base canard. No sooner do the children start piling stones than the hag and all her demons (I forgot to mention the demons, but they're there) start knocking them down as fast as the youngsters put them up.

Enter our hero, Jizo-sama.

Jizo is full of love and pity for the children. He drives the hag and her demons away. He takes the children in his arms and comforts them. And then, to keep the witch from finding them again, he hides them in the great sleeves of his kimono. If you see an image of Jizo, or a statue, or stone plaque, you'll notice those huge sleeves.

And if you stop at a statue by the road, place a stone before it —any stone will do—and utter the appropriate prayer, you lighten the labor of some youngster's soul when his time comes to approach the river of the dead.

Near Hakone, a mountain resort near Tokyo, there's a statue of Jizo said to be over a thousand years old and reputed to have been carved by Japan's leading Buddhist saint, one Kobo Daishi, teacher, traveler, painter, and sculptor who, among other things, invented the Japanese auxiliary writing known as *hiragana,* which we'll explain further in the chapter on language. Before Kobo Daishi's tomb in Nara there's a flame that's burned continuously for over a thousand years.

Hope you've enjoyed meeting our deities. Hope you'll recognize them when you see them again. If you stay any time at all in Japan, you will.

chapter four

the emperor

He is a quiet little man with a faintly weary air about him. He is, one suspects, happiest when alone with the fish and plant-life specimens he collects as an amateur marine biologist. It's unlikely that you would ever see him on the street, strolling along like an ordinary citizen, but if you did you would probably put him down as an amiable family man and a mildly hen-pecked husband.

Hirohito* was born in 1901 and he is the only ruler in the world who comes from an unbroken line of succession. He is, at this writing, the Emperor of Japan—an office as unique as the nation itself.

* One of the small difficulties foreigners run into when they refer to the emperor in the company of Japanese is the pronunciation of his name. English-speaking people tend to say Hee-ro-*hee*-to. In Japanese the stress is more nearly equal on all syllables so that to our ears the second syllable sounds a little more prominent—Hee-*ro*-hi-to. And the Tokyo accent gives this a special twist, so that what comes out is something like Hee-*roash*-to.

Most Westerners first became decidedly aware of Japan at the outset of World War II when the Allies found that this remote empire had suddenly become a tough and bitter foe. There was a great deal of hasty copy written about the Japanese character in those days, most of it colored by stereotyped notions of a "cruel and mysterious Orient," much of it half-truth or downright error. One of the more puzzling aspects of the Japanese was their relationship with their emperor whom, we were told, they regarded as divine—a living god. We readily accepted this dictum, I think, because it helped to explain some of the fanaticism and irrationality (from our viewpoint) that we encountered. It made sense out of the *banzai* charges and *kamikaze* attacks.

But just how deep does this concept of imperial divinity go? And what does the average modern Japanese think of his emperor—especially since Hirohito himself, shortly after World War II, took the trouble to announce to his people that he was *not* divine?

I think there's a great deal of understanding of the Japanese way of thinking to be gained by looking, even briefly, at the relationship between the citizen and the emperor.

history
and myth
The beginnings of the imperial line are shrouded in a miasma of legend—nobody really believes the story literally, but everybody accepts it for lack of a better image, perhaps as we accept Santa Claus or the legend of George Washington and the cherry tree.

The first emperor, legend-history tells us, was named Jimmu. He founded the empire in 660 B.C. This sounds factual enough, but the details of the story form a sort of creation myth.

The Sun Goddess had a grandson named Ninigi, and she sent him down from the Moor of Heaven, entrusting to him the three sacred symbols of the Imperial House: the Sword, the Mirror, and the Jewels. Prince Ninigi, presumably dropping from the sky, landed in Kyushu and established a headquarters there.

But the other islands of Japan were inhabited by scattered independent tribes who apparently hadn't heard of the Sun Goddess and her progeny. Several generations went by before these divine offspring were strong enough to subjugate the rest of the Japanese islands, and it was Prince Ninigi's great-grandson who finally mounted an expedition to the present site of Osaka and there fought a campaign that brought the greater part of Japan under his control.

His name was Jimmu and he was the first emperor of Japan.

There have been 124 emperors since. The present Crown Prince Akihito, who is the first of the line to marry a commoner, is slated to be the 125th.

the era system It is the reigns of the emperors that determine the old-style Japanese calendar. Everything dates from Jimmu (660 B.C.) and continues to the present day in a series of years and eras. The year A.D. 1961 is, by the old Japanese system, 3,021. This method is still used in many official and ceremonial matters, though our Western calendar exists with it side by side. This is only one of the multiple standards that make ordinary life so confusing for the average Japanese citizen.

But it gets even more complicated. With each emperor—and remember, there have been 124—there is a new era, with its own name. We are now in the Showa era. It began, automatically, upon the death of the Emperor Taisho, and the succession of the present emperor, Hirohito. Under certain circumstances you can use the era system to fix a given year—calling it the fifth year of Taisho, the third year of Showa, and so on. A year ordinarily starts on January 1. But Taisho died on December 25, 1926. From his death until the first of January was the first year of

Showa—a period of less than a week! On January 1, 1927, it was then the *second* year of Showa.

School children are required to memorize all 124 of the eras, which makes the study of history quite a task. Major earthquakes, for example, are listed by the era system. We're told that such cataclysms occurred in the thirteenth year of Hakuho, the seventh year of Meio, the first year of Keicho, and so on. Some Japanese can keep it all in their heads, but the average person has to refer to a table to pinpoint the time.

Incidentally, the names by which we know the emperors and their eras today are not the emperors' original names. A Japanese ruler, upon his death, receives a new name and he is forever after known by this. The average person forgets his real name and again would have to refer to special reference tables in order to learn it. As an example, an emperor named Goyozei reigned from A.D. 1596 to 1614, but he is now known as Keicho, and the years of his reign as the Keicho era. When the present emperor, Hirohito, dies, he too will be given a new historical name.

For many centuries the emperors of Japan were indeed remote figures, kept virtually as honored prisoners in their palaces, shielded from public view, while the real business of running the country was carried on by the shogun, a sort of combined prime minister and king, whose office was hereditary. Shoguns were occasionally overthrown, and new families took over. The emperor, however, always remained. His person was sacred. In some periods of Japanese history it meant death to so much as look upon him when he passed. Oddly, though, he seldom made any decisions of state, and these old emperors, in fact, in their pathetic seclusion, usually knew very little of what was actually going on in the country.

Things are quite different today, of course, but this is the tradition behind the concept of the emperor and his divinity.

meiji, the
strong man

The first of the really modern emperors was the strong man, Meiji, whose era lasted from A.D. 1868 to 1912. It was he who pushed the modernization and Westernization of Japan, turning her from a feudal to an industrial power in the space of a few decades, an achievement unparalleled in all of history. Throughout Japan today his name is still encountered: buildings, areas, corporations, and shrines are named after him (even milk and chocolate), so that we encounter "Meiji" in Japan as frequently as the names of Washington and Lincoln in the United States.

It was the emperor Meiji who made the imperial office more significant, more worldly than it had been for centuries and now one sees in perspective that it was Meiji who paved the way for Hirohito's eventual public renunciation of divinity shortly after World War II.

In 1888 Meiji had a new constitution formulated. This stated that the emperor was the true sovereign, the head of the army and navy, could issue imperial ordinances in place of laws, decide on the organization of the government, make war, peace, and treaties, and act in general as the unquestioned ruler of the country.

Meiji had a mind of his own, but his immediate descendants were not able to dominate the ruling cliques of the country as he had done. It is generally conceded by historians and commentators now that Hirohito was more or less pushed into the great war that was waged in his name and that led, after Japan's defeat, to the present constitution, which went into effect on May 3, 1947.

the emper-
or today

Japan's present monarch, in his functions, resembles the British monarch. He is a constitutional monarch. He is the symbolic rather than the

actual head of state, and under the new constitution the sover-
eignty of the people and a representative form of government are
recognized. He has no greater privileges, basically, than the
average citizen, and most of his acts are mere formalities.

No well-informed citizen of Japan today looks upon the emper-
or as divine, although he is ordinarily accorded a great deal of
respect and even affection as the symbol of the nation. Some older
people, in remote parts, are unable to grasp this new concept of
the "human" emperor and still regard him in the ancient way.
Occasionally, as you pass the Imperial Palace in Tokyo, you will
see groups of men and women working on the grounds, perhaps
gathering and disposing of litter. They have made special pilgrim-
ages from the country as an act of devotion. Often this is the only
long journey such people will take in all their lives, and they
both look forward to the trip and talk about it ever afterward.

On the opposite side of this scale you will find modern Japanese
who are downright critical of their emperor, and who will go so
far as to mock him or call for abolition of the office. But such people are exceptional; the average Japanese thrills warmly at the
sight of his ruler and follows the doings of the imperial family
with deepest interest.

Japan has prospered as a constitutional monarchy, and it's
probable that her people are happier and more secure these years
than ever before. The crown prince, presently to be the emperor,
is a modern young gentleman in every sense of the word. He was
educated by an American tutor, Mrs. Elizabeth Gray Vining, in
his early years. He has been abroad, and has visited more foreign
countries than any of the royal line before him. In his public
appearances he exhibits poise, graciousness, and charm that are
particularly appealing to Westerners and that doubtless evoke
affection from his future subjects.

Hirohito, the present emperor, says little about world and

state affairs; we glimpse him now and then on a balcony, waving his hat, smiling quietly, looking as though he wished the ordeal of public appearance would come to an end quickly. He is a likeable figure, somehow, and one wishes one could know him better. But the old tradition of divinity, though renounced, still forms a sort of barrier between him and ordinary people. It may be that Crown Prince Akihito and his descendants will destroy that barrier altogether.

chapter five

meet the samurai

The samurai don't exist any more, but if you're to understand present-day Japanese you'd best know about them. The reason is that down in the dark places of his heart nearly every Japanese man thinks of himself as a sort of samurai. This is almost a direct parallel of the American fantasy in which every U.S. male would emulate the heroic figure of the cowboy. Cowboy and samurai—sense their faults and virtues and you have practically and comparatively psychoanalyzed two nations.

The samurai was a professional warrior who stalked through Japan until a little less than a hundred years ago. He wore two swords, one short and one long. He never touched money. It was his right to lop off the head of anyone who didn't show him proper respect as he passed by.

The word "samurai" means one who remains on guard. There have been various names for this warrior class down through Japanese history, but this is now the generic term. Westerners tend to lump everything before the Meiji Reformation of the 1870's into the "feudal period" and this of course is an over-simplification, for Japan, since its first reliably recorded history, has developed a number of social structures. However, the general system of society that predominated before Meiji was rather like that of Europe in the Middle Ages, with land and titles hereditary, and lesser folk bound to nobles who owned the various fiefs. In our Western history the shining figure of this period was the knight. In Japan, it was the samurai.

He flowered at his fiercest for nearly a thousand years and was especially prominent on the Japanese scene during the last great line of shoguns, the Tokugawas, who ruled from about A.D. 1600 to the middle of the nineteenth century.

He had a rigid code of honor, from which was derived a philosophy known as Bushido, or the Way of the Warrior, and which was conveniently perverted in wartime, as many philosophies are, to become a basis for internal propaganda and an emotional stimulant.

Let us first look briefly at the social system that produced the samurai class.

The emperor was the national and religious symbol of old Japan, but the hereditary prime minister called the shogun really ran the country. Under the shogun came his high administrative officers, a cabinet of four or five elders, and a lesser council of junior elders. There were also censors, intelligence officers, and a large group of civil administrators called *bugyo* scattered throughout the country. These officials, however, were not necessarily considered nobility.

The next important hereditary rank below the shogun himself was that of *daimyo*. The word might be translated as earl or baron. The *daimyo* owned huge areas of land and ruled the people on them. They were the virtual monarchs of small, independent states and throughout Japanese history were frequently involved in bloody wars with each other. That was why each *daimyo* had to keep a corps of elite warriors in readiness—and these of course were the samurai.

Only nobles, doctors, teachers, and samurai could use a family name in those days. It is interesting to see how the common people were ranked: farmers came first, artisans second; bankers and merchants (who handled the money the samurai considered filthy) were last. Among the population were some slaves, taken in wars for the most part, who were tattooed on the face and hands as mark of ownership. There was a certain class of peasants bound to the land, and there were some farmers who owned the lands they worked.

Class status changed with the times, however. Japan in the sixteenth and seventeenth centuries began a short period of trade with the outside world; a Portuguese, a Dutch and, briefly, an English trading post were established on her shores and brought a certain amount of prosperity and a changeover from a rice to a money economy. The lowest class—bankers and merchants— began to grow rich. The old die-hards were now often shocked to see a wealthy storekeeper arrogantly giving orders to a carpenter or mason working for him, for artisans outranked him socially.

Another class that rose above its original status was that of the swordsmiths, undoubtedly because they were so valuable to the samurai. They were called *shokunin* and the more outstanding of them were heaped with honors, receiving a special title that was pronounced the same as daimyo, but written in different characters.

Before we look at the samurai in detail I think I should mention one curious class of untouchables, and a strange prejudice of the Japanese that exists even today. These pariahs were known in feudal times as *chori*. They lived in separate areas in the suburbs of large cities and traditionally were permitted only certain trades: night watchman, gravedigger, torturer, and executioner. Among them was another group, the *eta*, who usually worked in leather. They could not enter any shop except that of a dealer in footgear—an "unclean" commodity. The eta were called "things," not "people," and they were counted in the special numerals the Japanese use for counting animals. If you killed an eta it was not murder. You were fined, presumably for a sort of disturbance of the peace. Some say they were originally honored artisans in leather-working, butchering, and shoemaking, imported from the Asian mainland to fill a skilled manpower shortage, but that as the years passed they lost their favored position and became despised.

The untouchables exist today. How they came into being is still something of a mystery. There is no physical difference between them and other Japanese; they acquire their status simply through being born into an eta family. They are shunned by otherwise rational people who stoutly claim the ability to recognize eta by sight, though when pressed for the signs of recognition they're unable to do anything but mutter darkly. Often, when referring to eta, a Japanese will hold out four fingers, which signify the four legs of an animal, a gesture which also has various connotations of ill fortune. The foreigner is just as mystified when he asks what the eta did to deserve all this. Apparently they didn't do anything at all; they're just—well—they're just eta, that's all.

I have tried to show this feudal scene in some detail because this was the culture in which the fabulous samurai flourished. He was, as we have seen, a professional warrior attached to the court of a noble. When there was no fighting he had very little to do but practice the arts of war, make love, and otherwise amuse himself. His highest ideal was loyalty; he was supposed to give up his

life without hesitation for his lord, whenever it might become necessary. If he failed in an important task he was honor bound to take his own life. The method by which he did this is known popularly in the West as *hara-kiri,* but this is actually a vulgar term which in direct translation means "belly cutting." The better word is *seppuku.*

A rigid etiquette surrounds this entire process of formal suicide; it involves purification at a shrine as the first step, the donning of a ceremonial white kimono, the grasping of a special short knife with folded paper, and even a prescribed kneeling position for the completion of the act. The knife is thrust into the left side at belt level, drawn eight inches or so to the right, then turned and pulled upward for another few inches so that the stomach is laid open with an L-shaped cut. The idea of suicide makes the average Westerner shudder, but many Japanese are deeply moved by the concept and a good seppuku scene in a play or a movie will moisten every eye in the house.

Much of the illusion of the samurai's colorful character is in his costume. In different periods of history he had various ways of shaving his head, leaving ridges or topknots, and toy shops today sell samurai wigs in these various styles of hairdress. On formal occasions he wore a vest with huge, stiffened shoulder pieces; this was called a *kamishimo*. He sported a trouser-like split skirt known as a *hakama*. He wore a silk obi around his kimono and his two swords, long and short, were as much a badge of rank as they were weapons.

The samurai was usually very fastidious about his dress and never more so than just before a battle. The battlefield was his place of social fulfillment; a fight was his *raison d'être* and his most glorious moment. It was considered a great disgrace to be found carelessly dressed on a battlefield and when a samurai said he wouldn't be caught dead in such-and-such an outfit, he meant it literally.

The feeling is most eloquently stated in the story of Munehara Shimizu. His castle was put under siege and eventually it became clear that he would have to surrender. That meant seppuku, too. Before he began his ceremonial suicide he called in his retainers and told them to give him a clean, close shave. He knew his head would be taken to the enemy commander and he didn't want his foe to think that, in defense of his castle, he had been too busy to keep himself well groomed.

This potpourri of facts about the samurai, if I've selected properly, ought to add up to a certain *gestalt* in your mind. The ghosts of samurai still haunt modern, industrial Japan. The samurai way of life has a great unconscious influence upon the moral code of the Japanese male, just as the ideals of King Arthur's knights or the code of the cowboy lingers with his Western counterpart. Surely there were good, bad, and in-between samurai. Brave and cowardly. Honorable and perfidious. The swashbuckling aspect of the whole business is, of course, a monstrous fib. The fictional period of the samurai, like the Old West of Hollywood, never really existed.

Yet colorful they were, these samurai. And they had a code that in part resembles that of European knighthood. We Western peoples find a certain escape in our own tales of derring-do, and the Time of the Samurai is the delightful lie that sweeps the Japanese from the atomic complexities of the present to the more comfortably defined values of their costumed past.

chapter six

the forty-seven ronin

Much of a nation's character can be sensed from the favorite stories of its people. In the United States we have Daniel Boone and Davy Crockett; in England, King Arthur's knights. In Japan the tale that tells the most about the people is, I believe, a combined historical narrative and folk legend known as *Chushingura*.

Chushingura is the name of a Kabuki play made from the legend. Kabuki is the great stylized theater of Japan which we'll discuss in another chapter. The other title of the narrative is *"The Forty-Seven Ronin,"* and *ronin* means drifting ones, samurai without a master, and thus, by implication, without a positive direction or purpose in life.

In the original version of *Chushingura* (full title: *Kanadehon Chu-shingura*), there are dozens of major characters and sub-plots. The story is based on an actual incident of the early eighteenth century. Most Japanese are familiar with both the true story and the drama based upon it.

I have no space here for the entire tale, and if further study interests you, you may find whole books devoted to this one semi-legend and its significance. Even better, you may attend the Kabuki play which is shown, in whole or in part, every mid-winter to commemorate the attack and mass suicide which is the climax of the tale. There have also been a number of Japanese motion pictures made on the subject—a new one seems to come out every year.

I should like to introduce you to this story with a short radio play which has already been performed on the air several times. The plot is greatly simplified and forms a sketch rather than an exposition of the entire tale. But it may sharpen your curiosity to hear more of what is basically a corking good story.

the forty-seven samurai
A PLAY FOR RADIO

CHARACTERS

Oishi	*Male. Heroic, but sensitive, deep voice.*
Kira	*Male. Nasal, rather contemptuous, snobbish voice.*
Asano	*Male. Gentle, cultured voice.*
Voice	*Male. Nondescript—one of the retainers.*

Narrator

Extra crowd voices as needed.

(OPENS COLD)

VOICE: (*coming on*) Oishi! Oishi—are you awake?

OISHI: Hm? Oh . . . yes. I was resting. Still dark, I see. What time is it?

VOICE: Early morning. Look outside, Oishi. Snow.

OISHI: Yes. I see. Snow. And Kira won't expect us to attack in the snow, will he? Well . . . I suppose the time has come. How many are we now?

VOICE: Forty-seven.

OISHI: Forty-seven. Forty-seven masterless samurai. Forty-seven *ronin*. And after we take Kira's life—

VOICE: (*eagerly*) Yes?

OISHI: Forty-seven will die!

MUSIC: *Theme. (broad costume-drama music)*
Establish opening, then fade and hold under:

NARRATOR: This is the story of the forty-seven samurai. It is one of the most famous of all Japanese stories . . . it has been a favorite for two and a half centuries. It deals with the samurai code of honor . . . and in a larger sense . . . with social and moral relationships. Here is our version . . . simplified and adapted for radio . . . of the Forty-seven Samurai!

MUSIC: *Theme crosses to melancholy curtain mood. Hold under:*

OISHI: My name is Oishi.
This is the 14th year of Genroku, or,
As you would say in the Western world—
Seventeen hundred and one.
I am in a place called Yedo.
Later it is to be called Tokyo—
The City of the East.

MUSIC: *Sting effect, then under again for:*

OISHI: As you see me, Oishi . . . as you see me now,
I am hardly an admirable character.
I am a samurai . . . a warrior.
You know this by my dress; by the two swords
I carry in my sash.
I spend my time drinking and carousing . . .
Each day becoming more unkempt.
I have a purpose in all of this.
I am waiting. Waiting for . . . revenge.
Forty-six other samurai,
Like myself, in disguise,
Are also waiting here.
Waiting . . . *(fade off)* . . . in the city of the
East. . . .

MUSIC: *Out.*

NARRATOR: It all began in Kyoto, the ancient capital of Japan.
Oishi was the chief retainer to a noble named Asano.
The emperor told Asano to carry his imperial greet-
ings to the Shogun's palace in the City of the East.
The Shogun was the real leader of Japan—a prime
minister even more powerful than the emperor
himself.

Now Asano . . . though of noble birth . . . was
a simple man. He knew little of court etiquette and
cared less. To help him, a more sophisticated courtier,
named Kira, was to go along. Kira, however, was
a greedy man. . . .

KIRA: Now, Asano, I'll be delighted to help you when we
get to court! And I trust you'll be . . . shall we say
. . . properly grateful?

ASANO: Kira, if you're hinting about money again, save your

breath. I'm not going to bribe you to do what ought to be your simple duty. And I've a warning for you, Kira.

KIRA: A warning?

ASANO: I've seen you looking at my wife, Kira. I know what's in your mind.

KIRA: Asano! You're imagining things!

ASANO: I don't think so. And the warning still stands.

KIRA: Very well . . . if that's how you feel. We'll see what happens when we get to the capital!

NARRATOR: Kira, the experienced courtier, waited until they reached the Shogun's palace in the big city. Asano, of course, made a number of mistakes in etiquette. Kira gave him little help. And finally, in front of all the other nobles, Kira deliberately embarrassed the lord from the country.

KIRA: Honored lords and nobles! If you've any business to transact . . . you'd best do it with me! This bumpkin from the country knows nothing of good manners . . . or matters of state!

MUSIC: *Sting chord*.

ASANO: Kira!

KIRA: (*contemptuous*) Yes, Asano!

ASANO: I may know nothing of etiquette—but I know how to use this sword!

SOUND: *A scuffle*.

KIRA: Careful, Asano! Careful with that!

ASANO: This . . . is what you've been deserving all along! (*He grunts as he swings*)

NARRATOR: Kira dodged the blow. He was wounded only slightly. Then . . . Asano became cooler. He now realized the terrible thing he had done.

ASANO: I . . . I have drawn my sword in the palace!

Against all custom and law! Now, there's only one course . . . one honorable procedure!

MUSIC: *Sting and mood. Down for:*

NARRATOR: In Japanese it's called "seppuku" . . . sometimes "hara-kiri," or cutting of the belly. When you're in extreme disgrace, it is the only honorable course. This was what Asano was faced with now. But there is even more disgrace to come . . . indignity upon indignity . . .

KIRA: (*On echo*) It is the decree of the magistrates, Asano . . . that you commit suicide in the open air . . . upon a dirty mat!

NARRATOR: And when the terrible day came . . . Asano suffered one further degradation. Before he could plunge the knife into himself . . . one of the Shogun's guards lopped off his head . . . and denied him the privilege of suicide!

MUSIC: *Up to resolution, then out.*

NARRATOR: Not long afterward, a loyal retainer of Asano's, a man named Oishi . . . called a meeting of all the samurai who once had served the dead man.

SOUND: (*Cross in) Crowd mutter. Establish, then fade for:*

OISHI: Gentlemen! Gentlemen! Listen to me, gentlemen! Kira's villainy has brought a terrible disgrace to the house of Asano! I've called you here . . . to decide what's to be done!

VOICE: (*off slightly*) There's *nothing* to be done! I say we should all forget the past—disband!

OISHI: And I say not! I say we must avenge Asano! We must defy Kira! One day . . . we must place Kira's head . . . severed . . . on Asano's tomb!

VOICE: (*off*) Kira's too powerful! It's impossible!

OISHI: It's not impossible! And I have a plan! But it means that all who take part . . . must one day die . . . by their own hands!

SOUND: *Crowd reaction.*

OISHI: *(continuing)* Yes . . . by their own hands! Just as our master, Asano, died! Now, then! Those of you who wish to avenge Asano's death—remain here! The others may go! When they're gone . . . I'll tell you what I have in mind!

MUSIC: *Ominous bridge. Establish then hold under:*

NARRATOR: Forty-six agreed to Oishi's plan. Altogether,
            Forty-seven became ronin . . . masterless samurai.
            Ronin. Men of the waves. Drifting men.
            Men without a master . . . men without direction.
            But now, men bound together,
            By a common purpose.
            The warrior, Oishi, was their leader.
            Years passed. The forty-seven samurai,
            After many adventures, finally gathered in Edo—
            The City of the East.
            They had disguised themselves in various ways.
            Some had become shopkeepers . . . some crafts-men.
            Some tilled the soil . . . some were common la-borers.
            Oishi, their leader, posed as a ne'er-do-well,
            Spending his time in taverns,
            And places where the geisha gathered.
            Kira, the object of their revenge,
            Now lived in the City of the East.
            But his house was a fortress; attack seemed im-possible.

Until one dark morning when Oishi,
Received a visitor. . . .

VOICE: *(Coming on)* Oishi! Oishi! Are you awake?

OISHI: Hm? Oh, yes. I was resting. Still dark, I see. What time is it?

VOICE: Early morning. Look outside, Oishi. Snow.

OISHI: Yes, I see. Snow. And Kira won't expect us to attack in the snow, will he? Well . . . I suppose the time has come. We know everything about Kira's residence now. We know where every guard is placed. We'll strike tomorrow night. Are all forty-seven of us together?

VOICE: The others wait only the word.

OISHI: Are you sure . . . they wish to hear this word?

VOICE: Sir?

OISHI: It's different now, you know. Different than it was before.

VOICE: How is it different?

OISHI: We all came to Edo in disguise. We were samurai . . . but we took up various callings in order to live. Well . . . it seems that some of us have been successful at these new pursuits. Some of the men have found new lives for themselves. And some—

VOICE: Yes?

OISHI: Some have fallen in love.

VOICE: Nevertheless, Oishi . . . no one has forgotten our plan.

OISHI: Very well, then. But I hope one part of it is still quite clear.

VOICE: What's that, sir?

OISHI: When we defile Kira's house . . . when we take his life here in the city of the Shogun—

VOICE: Yes?

OISHI: When we bring his head to Asano's tomb—

VOICE: Yes, yes!

OISHI: Then we must kneel before a shrine. Then we must draw our short swords . . . and take our own lives!

VOICE: Yes, Oishi. We all remember that, too.

OISHI: Let us not forget it. It is the only way we may do this thing with honor.

VOICE: We'll not forget.

OISHI: And now . . . spread the word. We attack Kira's house tomorrow!

MUSIC: *Mood suggesting attack. Cross to:*

SOUND: *Shouting, clanking of swords.*

Fade for:

NARRATOR: And so the forty-seven samurai
             Stormed Kira's residence, which lay
             By a bridge in the City of the East.
             They surprised his bodyguards.
             They hunted him down.
             They killed him.
             His head was placed on Asano's tomb.
             And after that . . . after the deed,
             They calmly surrendered to the Shogun.
             The sentence upon them was passed.

VOICE II (ON ECHO):
             All forty-seven of the masterless samurai . . . are to die by their own hands!

VOICE: *Crash chord, trailing to sad-sweet mood. Hold under:*

NARRATOR: The small hill stands just south of Tokyo.
             You can see it there today. There is a temple,
             On the hill. And in its park,
             Stand forty-seven stones . . . the gravemarks

Of the loyal samurai.
In the sixteenth year of Genroku,
In the dead white winter of that year,
The forty-seven ronin gathered there,
Knelt . . . drew their swords . . . took their lives.
Their master . . . was avenged.

MUSIC: *Climax and resolve.*

NOTE: The forty-seven ronin are buried at Sengakuji Temple, about two miles southwest of Tokyo's Shiba Park. The temple can be reached by streetcar or bus from central Tokyo. Relics of the forty-seven samurai are preserved in one of the temple buildings.

chapter seven

the salaryman

Let us now come back to the present and meet an important Japanese citizen of modern times.

He supports a family on $102.50 per month. He lives in an attractive apartment, owns a washing machine, two radios, and five suits of clothes. He goes to the movies once a week, attends a geisha party about once every two weeks, and plays golf at least once a month. He lives a full and rewarding life and regards himself as a happy man. All on $102.50 every thirty days.

He is what Japanese call the "Salaryman."

This is the typical, middle-class, white-collar worker in Japan today, a man who does not ordinarily receive much attention in writings about Japan. How does he live—or, even more to the point, how does he do it on so small an income? The foreign visitor may find it difficult to learn much about the Salaryman, for he will be exposed mainly to wealthy or special-class Japanese on one hand, and to maids, guards, or delivery boys on the other. Yet the picture of the Salaryman affords a tremendous insight into modern Japan; he is certainly more significant in our time than the geisha, the samurai, or the cherry blossoms.

With this in mind I found a Salaryman and interviewed him. A most typical Salaryman, his is the expected story, the cliché that is nevertheless hard truth. The details are highly personal, and therefore I will give this Salaryman a fictitious name. Call him Ichiro Watanabe. That's about as close as you can get to saying John Smith in Japanese.

ichiro and his job   Ichiro Watanabe is thirty-four years old, married, has a daughter one year and seven months old, and is expecting another child in five months. He works for the Tokyo office of a large import and export company. His title is Assistant Section Chief, Non-Ferrous Metals Section. He works forty-four hours per week and has been with the company for twelve years.

Now, you have seen Ichiro Watanabe a hundred times on the streets of Japan's larger cities, perhaps hurrying to work in the morning with a briefcase under his arm, or reading his evening newspaper as he returns home on the crowded train at night. He is physically an urban type: compact, rather slender, neat, be-spectacled. He enjoys sports and has a healthy tan rather than a downtown pallor. His belt buckle bears the lacquered insignia of his college, a small pin in his lapel represents the company for which he works. He is apt to wear gray suits, quiet ties, always a white shirt freshly starched, and often the curious pearl-gray leather shoes that are popular with Japanese men.

On a typical morning at the office Ichiro will first read the cables that have come in from overseas points during the night, digest and answer correspondence, and then join a conference with the

boss and his colleagues, perhaps to determine how the firm should
bid to obtain a certain ICA contract in Spain, or some other plum
in some other part of the world. He has two male assistants—
younger men, of course—and in his entire section there are two
clerk-stenographers who handle all the correspondence and filing.
His firm occupies two floors of one of the large office buildings in
downtown Tokyo and his office is air-conditioned.

In the import-export business in Japan a knowledge of English
is absolutely necessary and Ichiro Watanabe, who studied English
at school for a total of six years, says he can "read almost anything,
write badly, and converse almost not at all." He would like to
have more practice in spoken English but finds little opportunity
for it and when, occasionally, he does find himself in a foreign
group, he is overcome with bashfulness and usually pretends that
he knows no English whatsoever.

finding his place Ichiro Watanabe was born in Tokyo but his parents
came, respectively, from the extreme southern and
northern parts of Japan. His father, now seventy-
three years old, is a well-to-do executive in a felt manufacturing
company and now has an income of approximately $417.00 per
month, which places him among the top ten percent of wage-
earners in Japan. Ichiro recalls a comfortable, happy childhood
with no particular problems. He attended elementary school for
six years, junior high school for three, senior high school for another
three, beginning this education at the age of six and ending it at
eighteen. He then entered Tokyo's Sophia University, majored in
Economics, and after four years was graduated in the upper third
of the class. Toward the end of World War II he was drafted into
the Japanese Army for three and a half months, but spent this
time in basic training and was discharged without ever having
left the home islands. His furthest trip was a vacation sojourn in

Manchuria during his student days. He has been to no other foreign countries.

After graduation from college Ichiro was introduced to his present company through his father's acquaintance with one of the executives. There was a brief oral interview, a mere formality, and he was given the job. He says that most such jobs are obtained through family or business connections rather than through competitive effort, although bosses will shy away from hiring an obvious incompetent, no matter what his connections.

The help-wanted columns of Japanese newspapers are not loaded with job opportunities, at least not in the white-collar field; the competition for employment is keen and Tokyo University sociologists estimate at this writing that only thirty percent of the college graduating force each year finds employment in appropriate professions.

Ichiro's starting salary with his company was ¥970 per month which, at the 1947 rate of exchange, was about $20.00. This was soon raised (because of inflation) to ¥3,000, which at that time equaled not much more.

Ichiro was pleased with his job from the start, though not particularly amazed to have found it, since he had expected as a matter of course that his father's influence would find some sort of employment for him and since this, in varying degrees, was also the assumption of most of his friends. He worked hard and conscientiously, not so much out of a desire to gain advancement as out of a natural, almost tribal instinct to conform to the patterns of his group and class. Since his father had helped him obtain the job, shirking or incompetence would have reflected disgrace upon his parent and, by implication, upon all his ancestors.

In order to demonstrate his cooperativeness in those early days with the company, Ichiro would often stay as much as an hour after closing time each day, or indulge in a kind of game with his co-workers to see who could arrive earliest and brightest of eye in the morning. Now that he has been with the company for twelve years he does not practice this kind of one-upmanship so often, but occasionally throws in extra time out of a lurking sense of the fitness of things.

no dull boy, ichiro In a Japanese company, however, all is not work. Parties, outings, theater trips, and other diversions are supplied for employees, and their frequency and lavishness depends upon the firm's prosperity. Even in bad times there is always one large outing a year for all the employees: perhaps a picnic in the suburbs of Tokyo, or perhaps a short trip by hired bus to one of the nearby hot springs or seashore resorts. On such an expedition the entire office crew will be quartered in a reserved hotel, usually of the old-style, Japanese-inn type, with married persons separated in their own rooms and unmarried people grouped together dormitory or roommate fashion.

And then there is the expense account. This nontaxable joy assumes even more importance in Japan than in the United States; it is the Japanese Salaryman's principal source of entertainment. If he is in a supervisory position, as Ichiro Watanabe is, he will act as host perhaps as often as twice a month to a client the company is anxious to infuse with good will. Even if he is a mere cog he will often be invited to go along on the various business parties sponsored by the company, though not so often as once a week; and if there are a great many employees in a section a fair boss will carefully rotate these opportunities so that everyone gets a chance.

Until recent years the usual expense-account affair was a geisha party, but golf has now become an increasingly popular method of entertaining. As Ichiro says: "It's healthier—and cheaper." Night clubs are also replacing geisha restaurants these days.

Whatever the occasion, the wives usually miss out on it. This is strictly for men, and the custom is a logical development of the geisha-party days. It shows no signs of dying out.

When a favored customer is to be entertained, Ichiro Watanabe takes him to any of several establishments that know his company and there he signs the bill, which is usually settled monthly. He is given an idea of what he may spend before he leaves, and this amount varies according to the importance of the client. The highest amount he has been permitted to spend so far is ¥30,000 or $83.30 in one evening. The expenses will include the establishment's bill, plus transportation for the evening, which is usually done by special taxis known as *"haiya,"* which, if you pronounce it in the Italian-vowel fashion, will readily disclose its derivation. This bill, too, is paid monthly.

mr. and mrs. salaryman   About once a week Ichiro Watanabe manages to have an evening of entertainment with his wife, and this is usually in the form of a movie. Every Sunday the Watanabes are in the habit of going for a walk through the Ginza, Tokyo's largest downtown shopping section, and at least once each summer they manage to take a trip to the country, either overnight or for several days. Ichiro's vacation time is calculated according to his length of service with the company and he has now accumulated thirty-six days.

His wife, Kimiko, has no particular objection to the frequent geisha parties and night-club sessions he necessarily attends. When asked if this is because she trusts her husband, her face assumes an expression of mild surprise, as though she never had thought to ask herself this question before. Of course she trusts her husband. She appears to regard the entire system as part of the natural order of things, like sunshine, rain, and earthquakes.

Ichiro Watanabe, like a great many modern Japanese young

men, chose his own wife rather than having his marriage arranged by parents—or at least he had a certain degree of choice in the matter. After he had been working for some time with his company, both his father and the boss, out of paternal interest, made frequent attempts to arrange a marriage for him. He was shown photographs of at least ten eligible young ladies over a period of several years, and numerous meetings, carefully staged to look accidental (though all parties concerned knew perfectly well they were not), were arranged. Each time Ichiro politely but firmly let it be known that he was not interested in the candidate presented, and this usually took the form of a trickling-off period, during which he saw, phoned, or referred to the young lady less and less frequently.

One day a cousin who lived in Nara, some three hundred miles distant, wrote to Ichiro that he had found a girl he thought might be suitable. Ichiro was skeptical but, no man to leave a stone unturned, journeyed to Nara for what was ostensibly a family visit. His mother accompanied him on this trip. The meeting took place in a hotel and was heavily chaperoned, since not only Ichiro's mother attended, but various members of both the cousin's and the girl's families.

At first the principals merely gathered in the hotel lobby, sat, and talked politely. Finally, by tacit and mutual agreement, an "alone time" was arranged for the two young people. Ichiro and Kimiko first walked a bit in the garden of the hotel and then, as the amiability between them seemed to grow, extended their stroll into the town, which is famous for its ancient temples, shrines, and pagodas. As it turned out, they walked from 1:30 to 6:00 p.m. When they finally returned, the family members had assumed from the duration of their absence that things were going well. Everyone trooped into the hotel for dinner. Ichiro did not make a flat declaration that he was satisfied with Kimiko. It was all sensed by everyone, rather, and the small talk that followed touched on every subject imaginable except the betrothal.

Ichiro says: "I knew I'd marry Kimiko before we left the garden. I wanted my wife to have some kind of cultural pursuit, and to be almost a professional at it. Kimiko is an excellent Japanese classical dancer—besides, of course, being an excellent wife."

Mrs. Watanabe has the petite, self-effacing charm of most Japanese young women. She is quite pretty, though when you say so Ichiro becomes modest and bashful and answers, in a half bantering tone: "Oh, I don't think so. . . ."

home life   The newlyweds lived at first with Ichiro's parents, but spent the necessary year or so searching for ideal quarters in housing-short Tokyo. They were finally able to obtain a government-built apartment through the lottery system governing tenancy of these housing units. Ichiro entered his name on the list and each month anxiously waited to hear if his had been drawn. When the lucky day came, the Watanabes acquired a two-floor apartment consisting of three rooms, kitchen, and bath. The room floors are of *tatami,* or Japanese mats, but the Watanabes prefer to furnish their place in what might be called "semi-Western" style. They have beds instead of the usual double mattresses spread on the woven floors. They have a few chairs in the living room, although they usually squat on the floor around a low table when they have social gatherings. They have a flush toilet, but it is not Japanese style, or set into the floor. All this costs them ¥6,150 or $17.08 per month, plus an extra eighty-three cents for janitor charges.

worldly   In the short time they have been married, the
treasures   Watanabes have managed to save money and also to acquire a fair amount of goods. They own a

small electric refrigerator of Japanese manufacture that sells for $163.90. Ichiro managed, however, to buy this at a twenty percent discount through his company connections. He obtained his $80.60 washing machine in the same manner. Next, he plans to own a vacuum cleaner and a television set. He already owns two radios. Before these are bought, however, he thinks he may try to get a piano so that his daughter can study. The daughter is only nineteen months old but he is convinced that she will be musical, largely because his own hobby is music and because his older brother was once a minor opera singer.

The piano (or perhaps the TV or the vacuum cleaner) will probably be bought at the end of the year when Ichiro receives his usual bonus from the company. These bonuses come in June and December, and their amounts vary according to the prosperity of the company. For the last several years he has received, each time, about two and a half months' pay. His basic salary is ¥32,500. About ¥2,500 each month is taken out for taxes, which leaves the U.S. equivalent of $83.30 take-home pay.

Most of Ichiro's job expenses are in the form of clothes and transportation. He believes he spends a little more than the average person on the former because he is a fastidious dresser. He spends thirty-three cents each day to get to work and back. He lives approximately fifteen miles from the center of Tokyo and travels by both train and bus. It takes him a little more than an hour each way.

Although Ichiro, like any Salaryman, makes only a small budgetary allowance for entertainment and relies on the company to supply most of it, he has managed to put some rewarding time into hobbies. He plays the piano *s'koshi*—a little. He sang in the glee club at college and still meets now and then for a musical session with an alumni group. Company golf has given him an enthusiasm for the game and he shoots about a hundred for eighteen holes. He owns two sets of clubs; an old outfit which his wife sometimes uses, and a newer set of American-made clubs which cost him $111.00 and of which he is very proud.

future
dreams
Ichiro Watanabe does not hope to be a Salaryman all his life. His dream, as a matter of fact, is to open up his own import-export business some day. This, when he mentions it to friends, sometimes shakes their traditional sense of Japanese loyalty which, in feudal days, was directed toward one's lord and in modern times is accorded to one's employer. To his friends, however, Ichiro explains that although he got his job in the first place by influence, his connections are not sufficiently strong ever to allow him to become a big executive with the firm. The top posts go to nephews and cousins.

Ichiro is not only planning, but saving for the future. He owns a small amount of stock in the company for which he works. He has life insurance policies, each in the amount of approximately a thousand dollars, on all three members of his family. He has about ¥50,000, or $138.90, in a savings account.

Ichiro Watanabe is busy and happy. He expects neither catastrophe, nor a serious halt in the forward march of his country's increasing prosperity. In politics he follows Japan's more conservative party, the Liberal Democrats, but often votes independently, for the man rather than for his affiliations. He is not in favor of revoking the "no war" clause in Japan's constitution. He likes Americans but has ambivalent feelings about their presence here in the form of Security Forces; he would rather see them as ordinary guests, under no military aegis. But at the same time he is quite aware that playing host to the U.S. Forces has become one of Japan's major industries, and he would not like to see the vast yearly U.S. expenditures withdrawn from his country's economy.

He would be in favor of increased trade between his country

and Communist China, but admits that this is probably colored by the fact that he works in the import-export business.

Ichiro hopes some day to travel more. He wants to see France, the United States, and England, in that order. He thinks that one of the factors which still make Japanese, even in this shrinking world, seem "different" is that so few of them have had the chance to leave their islands and see other places. But like nearly all Japanese he supposes that if and when he does travel he will most miss his daily ration of Japanese rice and some of the special Japanese foods he enjoys, such as raw tuna, sliced lotus roots, and real Japanese soy sauce.

I gathered all these facts from Ichiro Watanabe as we sat at a long lunch in a Chinese restaurant in downtown Tokyo. We had a private room and spent the time cross-legged on the mats at a low table. It was a warm day and we removed our jackets and ties. This imparted a certain informality to the occasion and, I think, contributed to a certain amiability between us. I had already asked Ichiro a number of what most Japanese would regard as highly personal questions, and this, too, perhaps broke the ice a bit.

Finally I said: "I'm sure you have a pretty good picture of your American middle-class counterpart. You know how much he owns. Big automobile, refrigerator, hi-fi set, all the rest. Do you ever get envious?"

He smiled. "American people," he said, "have many things. But sometimes—" and his smile became apologetic—"they do not know what to do with them."

chapter eight

people's pets

You may have thought that animals, less complicated creatures than we, have an international language to avoid the misunderstandings that have plagued humans since the Tower of Babel. But I don't believe this is so. The kernel of my suspicion is a fact I happen to have come across, namely that Japanese dogs bark in Japanese.

English and American dogs say: "Bow-wow!"

Japanese dogs say: *"Wan!"*

You may recall a Walt Disney cartoon motion picture of some years ago that dealt with the adventures of a number of dogs. It was called "The Lady and the Tramp." The direct translation of this title made little sense in Japanese and so it became, on

Tokyo and Osaka marquees: *Wan-Wan Monogatari*—or, Bow-Wow Tales.

In appearance Japanese dogs and cats are not too different from those we know in the Western world, and if you're a pet fancier you should be right at home in Japan. Japanese people are extremely fond of pets and the already crowded islands are well populated with domestic animals. As you look around, you will notice a great many familiar breeds—German shepherds, spitzes, collies, and so on—because foreign dogs are decidedly popular in Japan, and for several decades preceding World War II they threatened to replace native breeds completely. But there are native Japanese varieties too, and some of them are fine animals by any standards.

the akita   The best-known Japanese breed of dog is the Akita, pronounced as though the accent were on the first syllable. Its name comes from Akita Prefecture, which is in the northern part of Honshu, Japan's main island. Recently, Akita dogs have become popular with foreigners. With the increased demand their value has soared accordingly, so that a good Akita pup will cost you the equivalent of a hundred American dollars or more. A number of them have been taken to the United States and Europe, and an Akita-fanciers' association has been formed in America to promote the breed.

The Akita is a handsome dog. His coloring—gray, buff, brown, with sometimes a black muzzle—resembles that of a German shepherd. He stands about as high as a shepherd but is much heavier and stronger, and some would say that he resembles the Eskimo husky, with overtones of the chow in his conformation. He has a tendency to be a one-man dog, and his principal characteristic is his faith and devotion to his master.

the tosa   Another native breed, somewhat smaller than an Akita, is called the Tosa. He's considered the best fighting dog in Japan. Several hundred years ago dog fighting was a popular sport in the islands. A certain regent of Japan, one Takatori Hojo, was so fond of dogs that he kept five thousand on hand just as fighters. The practice has pretty much died out in modern times, although you can still run across an occasional dog fight in remote rural communities.

There was another rather barbarous practice in feudal days, known as the dog chase. A hundred or so Tosas were released and horsemen with bows and arrows would chase after them, shooting. Anything like that today would arouse a lot of protest from dog lovers all over Japan. There's a Japan Society for the Prevention of Cruelty to Animals, very active in good works here, as in other countries.

the chin   If your taste doesn't run to one-man or fighting dogs there's a fine lap-dweller bred in Japan and known as the Chin. He's one of the oldest of the island breeds. He looks rather like a cross between a spaniel and a Pekingese; he's usually bright, amiable, and easily trained. Ordinarily he's a black and white dog weighing around five pounds. He's not as popular as the other two species, so is a little rarer and also fairly expensive. There must be very few, if any, Chin in Europe or America, and that ought to make him a good conversation piece to take home.

the wonderful mixed breeds   Japan is also full of mongrels of all shapes and sizes. I've owned several, having acquired them (or perhaps they acquired me) in the usual accidental ways, and I find them most satisfactory and invariably bilingual. One of the delightful by-products of mongrel ownership is the fun of taking such a dog to the United States and there swearing that he is genuine Shimbashi noodle terrier or something equally outrageous.

Now, since Japanese houses are usually no-shoe houses, dogs are seldom brought inside. Most of them are trained to stay in the small entrance vestibule called the *genkan* or, more often, in dog houses outside. But big dogs require exercise and running space, and in crowded Japan this can be a problem. One favorite way to exercise them is to go bike riding with the dog running alongside on a leash. How the animal is trained to do this, I don't know; I've tried it and gained only skinned knees and elbows. But if you've the patience Japanese dog owners have, you'll probably be able to take part in this sport.

Japanese dogs usually recognize foreigners as people not quite like their owners, and will often bark at Westerners who go by, ignoring any nearby Japanese. Doubtless our smell is different. As a matter of fact you will notice, after a short time in Japan, that Japanese ordinarily have a less strong body odor than Caucasians and among themselves speak of the characteristic aura surrounding Europeans and Americans as "butterfat smell." Of course if you, a foreigner, own a Japanese dog he'll get used to *your* smell and bark at Japanese.

dogs and superstition
Dog-lovers, like most hobbyists, find much to talk about when they get together. In Japan there are even a number of superstitions connected with dogs. One has to do with childbirth. In the Orient, years and days are often named after the twelve signs of the ancient Zodiac—snake, monkey, bull, boar, rabbit, and so on. One of these signs is that of the dog. On the day of the dog, which comes every thirteen days, a woman bearing a child will often put a special belt on her dog, because a canine is known for its

easy delivery and by this she hopes to lessen the difficulty of her own parturition. Sometimes, for the same reason, an expectant mother will place a small model of a dog near her bed.

Japanese dogs get into religion, too. There are dog shrines and dog temples. In Tokyo alone there are at least three such places where dogs and cats are buried. One, built exclusively for canine interment, is called Kembyo-ji . . . another, Saishin-ji, has some forty thousand gravestones erected over the remains of cats and dogs, each bearing the animal's name. Here a regular Buddhist service is conducted at the time of burial.

dog stories There are hundreds of dog yarns in Japan. Here is one about a dog named Maru. It's supposed to be true and there exists today a hundred-year-old gravestone marking this dog's burial place.

A samurai named Ishiwara received a rather special present from the lord of his manor—a number of rare, pedigreed rabbits. Ishiwara also had a dog named Maru, a favorite pet and faithful companion. At first Maru appeared to show no more than a mild, passing curiosity about the rabbits.

One morning Ishiwara came to the cage and found a rabbit missing. Then, three mornings in succession, three more disappeared. Before long, seven were gone.

Now, the rabbits had been a gift, and to lose such a gift was considered an act of disloyalty or faithlessness, the implication being that Ishiwara hadn't thought highly enough of the rabbits to take proper care of them. He looked all around for the rabbit thief. Finally he could think of no one but his favorite dog, Maru. He drove Maru out into the cold of night, in the dead of winter, telling him, one imagines, never to sniff at his stone lanterns again.

That night, very late, Ishiwara heard the noise of a violent struggle in the garden. He went outside with a lighted candle. To his surprise he found three dead wolves in the snow. Maru was biting at the throat of a fourth, and by the time he'd finished him off was himself almost dead from the wounds he'd received. Ishiwara gathered the dog into his arms and, with tears in his eyes, apologized for suspecting him and driving him out. Maru died and Ishiwara buried him in the garden.

A somewhat more legendary tale about dogs concerns Kobo Daishi, the famed teacher and Buddhist saint of Japan. Once Kobo Daishi went on a pilgrimage to Matsuyama on the island of Shikoku. He stopped overnight at a farmer's house and the farmer said: "We're troubled here with wild boars. They come every night and uproot our garden. We'd appreciate it if you'd give us a charm against them."

Kobo Daishi took up a brush and painted something on a piece of paper. Folding this, he handed it to the farmer and told him to hang it in his garden. The farmer did this as soon as Kobo Daishi had left.

That night, and on succeeding nights, the charm worked; the wild boars never came near the garden. Finally the farmer became curious about it and wondered what Kobo Daishi had sketched on the paper. When he opened it he simply saw the picture of a dog. But hardly had he glimpsed it before the image of the dog flew away. This image is now rather well known in Japan as *Inu-kami,* or dog spirit, and is regarded as a minor deity.

More than any other dog quality, faithfulness seems to be what appeals to most Japanese people. There are a number of statues of dogs scattered throughout Japan but perhaps the most famous is a life-size bronze of a pooch called Hachiko. It stands today in the plaza of Shibuya Station in Tokyo. Hachiko was a dog of modern times and before World War II accompanied his master every morning to Shibuya Station and waited there until he returned from work. One day the master was drafted into the army and didn't return. Hachiko still waited, day after day. Passersby noticed him there and often fed him. He became a familiar fixture at the station. The master was killed in the war and never did return, but Hachiko refused to move from the plaza for many years. When the dog finally died an association of Shibuya merchants erected the statue in his honor and today it is a favorite meeting place for young lovers who presumably hope to acquire some of Hachiko's faithfulness in their future lives with each other.

minority report—cats
We've given a lot of time to dog lovers, who probably outnumber cat lovers, but for the sake of those individualists (I'm one) who appreciate the feline species, let's see how cats are regarded in Japan. The first thing you'll notice about Japanese cats is that they almost invariably have short tails. I've been asked hundreds of times: "Are they born this way, or are the tails cut?" They are cut. Long-tailed cats are credited with supernatural powers and can turn into witches and warlocks and such, and do you harm. (But even as I write this a friend of mine insists that his cat has just had a litter of five, all with short tails. It goes against all I've been taught about genetics, but I feel I have to present the case, in fairness.)

Most Japanese cats are of the alley variety. The pedigreed animals—Persian, Siamese, etc.—are usually imported. If you find a cat of three colors, you're in luck, say the Japanese. Seagoing people especially like to have a three-colored cat aboard ship. It keeps the devils away and protects the vessel from storms. When a cat uses its paw to wash its face, that means it's going to rain. This gesture of the cat is also similar to a beckoning of welcome, for the Japanese, like the American Indians, swoop the hand downward to beckon. There's a popular toy cat you see nearly everywhere in Japan with his paw raised in such a gesture. He is called *Maneki-neko,* or Beckoning Cat. Since he has been associated with shopkeepers for some time, he's considered to be skilled in finance and has become a symbol of saving. In Japan, children get cat banks instead of piggy banks.

And now, one more odd and, I suppose, fairly useless fact. Japanese cats speak in Japanese, too. Instead of Mee-ow they say *Niao.* And while we're on this subject, here's a full table of what animals say in Japan:

ANIMAL	ENGLISH	JAPANESE
Dog	Bow-wow	Wan-wan
Cat	Meeow	Niao
Rooster	Cock-a-doodle-doo	Ko-ke-kok-koh!
Chick	Peep-peep	Pio-pio
Horse	Wheeeee!	Hi-hin!
Cow	Moo	Moh
Pig	Oink	Bu-bu
Mouse	Squeak	Chu-chu
Frog	Garrump!	Gerro-gerro
Sparrow	Peep-peep	Chee-chee
Crow	Caw! Caw!	Kah! Kah!

PART TWO

places

chapter nine

the famed resorts

I know—you want to go to the out-of-the way places. Not the usual tourist traps. You want to be Stanley and Livingstone and Richard Halliburton. And later in this book, indeed, later in this chapter, we'll deal with such spots in Japan. But first let's face it—there are musts. The old Japan hands have been to the places everyone talks about, so you might as well take them in, too. The "must" resorts are like platitudes: not very original, but with a definite value nevertheless. Otherwise they wouldn't have remained popular so long.

nikko   Nikko is the prime example. "Never say *kekko* (beautiful) till you've seen Nikko." You'll hear that in Japan until you're ready to scream at the next person who quotes it. And if you listen to the usual build-up, which praises Nikko in superlatives but doesn't go into much actual detail, you'll probably be just a wee bit disappointed when you finally see the place. However, if you approach Nikko for what it is—a truly beautiful countryside cradling a number of unique shrines and historic spots—your visit will be altogether rewarding.

Nikko itself is a town of about 35,000, which makes it look smaller than a U.S. city of comparable size. It's not the town you go to see; it's the sights of the surrounding area.

The Nikko complex of attractions is between two and three hours north of Tokyo by train, perhaps four or five hours by automobile. On the whole the roads are good, though at this writing there are short, rough stretches, especially where the road is being repaired or newly built. The train is by far the most comfortable way to go, with a special "Romance Car" leaving Asak'sa Station in the northern quarter of Tokyo. This train gets its name from the plush double seats that look as though they were made to accommodate a pair of sweethearts, and just to improve the atmosphere soft, sweet music is played on the loudspeaker as you travel, interrupted now and then by a sweet-voiced young lady who calls attention to the passing points of interest. You can get to Asak'sa Station (if you can pronounce it) from downtown Tokyo for about ¥300 by cab, or, if you're traveling under Spartan rules, you can take the subway from any station along the Ginza. Asak'sa is at the end of the line.

The train brings you to the little town of Nikko, which nestles against a cluster of mountains. In the town itself a number of shops sell *omiyage,* the omnipresent souvenirs of Japan, and the best things to buy here are objects made of wood from the surrounding country. Carved tables and cherry-wood bowls are especially handsome.

Now that you're here there are two main general areas to visit. The first is the Toshogu Shrine and the various other shrines and temples near it. The second area is up in the mountains, and includes one of Japan's most spectacular waterfalls—Kegon Falls—and a large, high lake, Chuzenji.

You take in the shrines and temples first. They're within long walking distance, but you may wish instead to take a bus or taxi from the station, both of which are available. You climb the town's long, ascending main street and the first sight is one of the loveliest vermilion bridges in Japan. It's called Mihashi and it crosses the River Daiya. Scarcely a travelogue on Japan is filmed without it, and you'll want your own picture, I'm sure. You'll not be surprised to hear that there's a legend that goes with the bridge. We'll give it to you quickly. Back in A.D. 800, a Buddhist priest named Shodo was the first to climb the big mountain that towers over Nikko. During this original expedition, he found his way barred by the river. He prayed. A spirit appeared, made a bridge of two dragons across the river. A shrine to this spirit stands today on the left bank. Under good sunny conditions, use Kodachrome, f. 5.6 at 1/50th, to record it on film.

On the other side of the bridge a number of winding walks lead you through a lovely, hushed parklike area filled with shrines and temples. A gilded statue of Priest Shodo greets you before you've gone far. Next is the Rin-noji Temple, noted for its three Buddhist images, one crowned with a horse's head, another bearing a thousand hands.

Turn right at the temple. You now pass through one of the largest torii, or shrine gateways, in Japan. It's made of stone, the archway is over twenty-five feet high, and it was built in 1618. It marks the entrance to the famed Toshogu Shrine, which was built into its present state of magnificence in the early seventeenth century to commemorate one of Japan's greatest shoguns, Ieyasu, founder of the Tokugawa line. Just beyond the gateway is a five-storied pagoda, one hundred feet high.

A little further on, at the front gate, stand two of the most exciting statues you'll find in these islands. They're a pair of grotesque, fiercely grimacing characters who are called, in Buddhist terminology, *Devas*. One represents Indra, the other Brahma. These two are lacquered in bright vermilion and are deliberately made to look repulsive so that evil spirits will be frightened away from the temple gate.

Now, within the temple grounds, you'll find a number of interesting buildings, all in the ancient, rather Chinese style of architecture which might be called Japan Temple. They're full of curlicues, carvings, and giltwork. Probably you'll be most interested by a small structure which is called the Sacred Stable, and was built to shelter the ghostly horses of the temple deities, for it is here that we find the original three wise monkeys whose philosophy of see, speak, and hear no evil has caught the fancy of the whole world.

The monkeys are relief carvings over the door of the stable, and they're just a little disappointing. They don't look like the statuettes they've inspired. Know why they're on the stables? The monkey, according to the ancient Chinese, is supposed to protect horses from illness. Whatever you think of the original trio, you'll certainly want to buy one of those little paperweights of the three wise monkeys to take home from Nikko. They're on sale all over the place, in various sizes and materials, from twenty-eight cents to ten dollars or more.

There's an insignificant building beside the stables that I think is even more interesting. You know how the cowboys in the old West sometimes had to park their six-shooters at the door? Well, the same precaution evidently applied to the ancient samurai. This house is where they were supposed to leave their swords when they visited the shrine.

Broad steps now take you to three more shrine structures, a bell tower, a drum tower, and the Yakushido. This last is a large room with a dragon painted on the ceiling. For a small fee you can go inside, stand under the dragon's head, clap your hands, and, through some acoustical freak, hear the dragon groan. He doesn't really groan much, but it's fun to do it anyway.

The walkway continues through and past other interesting structures. You finally come to the grave of Ieyasu, the first of the Tokugawas, who was the first shogun to really unify Japan, and who actually took steps back in A.D. 1600 to open the country to the Western world. Unfortunately it was closed again by his son, Hidetada, who martyred a number of Christians in the process.

You can spend a good day in the area of temples and shrines, especially if you're fond of taking pictures, though I recommend flash equipment for the frequent shaded and dark places. Or you can get a sufficient impression in half a day (the purists will give me an argument on this), then move on to the mountain, lake, and waterfall.

Bus or taxi will take you up the mountain. It's a lovely, winding drive over a modern road. At one point there's an exciting cable-car ride to a nearby peak where the view is magnificent. Then . . . Kegon Falls offers a sight you'll never forget. The falls are over three hundred feet high and you can look at them from the top, or take an elevator to the mist-sprayed rocks below. They're noted as a spot for lovers' suicides.

Eleven and a half miles west (and up) from the town of Nikko is Chuzenji Lake, a vast and beautiful watery basin with several inns, hotels, and resort houses along its margin. Here we meet Priest Shodo again; his grave is on an islet in the lake. Boating and fishing are available. In the winter a nearby road leads to one of the best ski areas in Japan. Modern tows available.

This is Nikko, and now you have the right to say *kekko*.

kamakura   The big cliché at Kamakura is the huge statue of Buddha called the Daibutsu, probably the most photographed piece of sculpture in the world. But to leave Japan without your own snap of the great Buddha would be as disappointing as leaving Atlantic City without a box of saltwater taffy.

Kamakura is only an hour or so south of Tokyo by train. It's at once an historical site and a beach resort. It's also easy to reach by motor car from Tokyo, if you can find your way through Yokohama, a feat that sometimes gives pause to qualified navigators. One route now solves this by taking you on a fine new toll road. Kamakura has ninety thousand people, ninety temples, and forty shrines. It has a beach of fine sand, packed with humanity on summer weekends and lined with temporary reed pavilions where you may change your bathing suit, buy beer, or shoot arrows at targets. If you tire of swimming there are boatmen who will take you out into the bay in skiffs. There are also rickshaw in the town —one of the few places in Japan where you may still find them.

The main shrine to see in Kamakura is the Hachiman Shrine. It's within walking distance of the station. Exit at the main town plaza, go slightly downhill for a block and turn to your left on the big street. The Hachiman Shrine is straight ahead. Beautiful grounds . . . bright red torii . . . and a lovely arched bridge. The shrine is dedicated to Hachiman, the god of war. He was really the son of the Empress Jingu (A.D. 201–269), whose somewhat vigorous foreign policy gave us our English word *jingoism*. Hachiman was later deified and has a number of shrines throughout Japan dedicated to him. He is said to have lived 110 years.

Each mid-September, at this Hachiman Shrine, there's a spectacular demonstration of archery on horseback. The art and practice is called *yabusame,* and it's performed in costumes of what is called the Kamakura period, a span of several centuries following the twelfth century A.D., when the shoguns in power made Kamakura their headquarters.

The other compulsory sight at Kamakura is the huge statue of Buddha we have mentioned. To reach the Daibutsu you take a streetcar from Kamakura Station for several minutes to a stop called Hase (Hah'-say). A short walk from the tram stop takes you to a park in which the big Buddha stands—or rather, sits in contemplation. He is of cast bronze. He is forty-two feet, four inches high. The symbolic "third eye" between his eyebrows is seven and a quarter inches in diameter.

Daibutsu is one of two huge Buddhas in Japan. The one in Nara, an ancient city near the erstwhile capital of Kyoto in western Japan, is slightly larger, but sits in a huge shelter and is much more difficult to photograph. Daibutsu was originally a wooden image which was destroyed by a storm in A.D. 1248. It, too, was enclosed in a temple, but that was swept away by a tidal wave in A.D. 1495, leaving the image intact. You can go inside Daibutsu and climb up to his head for a small fee.

enoshima In good conscience I cannot let you leave Kamakura without urging you to drive or ride a bus a few miles further down the bay to the lovely, unique little shore town of Enoshima. Enoshima is really an island a few hundred yards out from the shore, reached by a long causeway, which you cross for a tiny fee. It's as though a small and delectable mountain had been planted in the water there. The island is full of climbing walks, shrines, inns, and intriguing little shops filled largely with souvenirs made of mother-of-pearl. There's a small zoo and observation tower on the crest of the mountain. On the other side of the island, perhaps fifteen or twenty minutes by foot, there's a most unusual shrine in a natural cave.

Enoshima, by the way, is the scene of most of the action—the salacious action, at any rate—of what I believe is the best book ever written by a foreigner about Japan: *The Honorable Picnic,* by Thomas Raucat.

The little town on the shore is called Katase and you'll find a number of attractions here, too. There's a big aquarium and a marineland filled with whales and porpoises. Feeding times occur throughout the day and you may purchase a can of fish and, if you're brave enough, stand on a platform while the dolphins leap seven or eight feet to snatch the tidbits out of your hand. The beach is fine. There are fishing boats and plenty of inns and hotels if you want to stay overnight.

Both on shore and out on the island you'll find little shops where you can paint your own designs on clay dishware and then have it glazed while you wait. Plates, cups, and ashtrays from these places make fine souvenirs. The Japanese people will probably put you to shame, however, with their natural artistic ability and skill with a brush. You can solve this by sort of hunching over whatever you're painting on the dish so that no one can see what you are doing.

If you're any kind of a gourmet the thing to buy in Enoshima is a shellfish called *sazae* (sah-zah-ay') which the dictionary tells me is a "wreath-shell clam" in English, but which I've never seen sold as food in America. Probably you'll have to get a Japanese cook to do it up properly for you: it's cut into pieces and cooked in a sauce in its own shell. Vendors sell these as well as conventional clams all along the streets and causeway, or you can taste one properly cooked in any of the dozens of restaurants throughout the area. Delicious.

hakone   Let's go up into the mountains again.

Fuji, the lovely, the perfect mountain, rises from a cluster of smaller peaks in an area seventy miles or so south of Tokyo. This area is now a national park, filled with exquisite landscapes and dotted with hot springs that gush from the innards of the earth, full of strong smells and strange vapors. Here there is also one of Japan's loveliest lakes—Ashinoko, sometimes called Lake Hakone.

The road from the capital is fine all the way. Train and bus service from Tokyo or Yokohama is quick and comfortable. As the winding highway climbs toward the lake there are dozens of other little towns and hot spring sites worth seeing. And you should stop and see them more than in passing. The lake itself is two thousand feet above sea level, and from its shores, or from surrounding eminences, you can see Fuji's crest in magnificent vistas on clear days. There's a passenger boat to take you on a tour of the lake. Inns, souvenir shops, caravanserais abound.

Hotels are both Japanese and Western style. Some are expensive, some moderately priced. Nearly all offer hot-spring baths in exquisite tiled pools into which the magic water is piped from the mountain. Japanese go to such places for the same reasons that people in Europe or America seek out spas—they believe that a good hot soak takes out the aches and pains. And so it does, or seems to.

To reach Hakone by motor from Tokyo you drive in a generally west and south direction along the shore of the great Sagami Bay until you come to a city called Odawara, and here you follow the main road up into the highlands. However, if you turn left and south at Odawara . . . or perhaps if you continue on the highway through Hakone and over the mountains . . . you will come eventually to the Riviera of Japan and the shore resort that is dedicated to pleasure. This is . . . Atami.

atami   Glittering is the word for Atami. It glitters from the air at night; it glitters as you approach it from the hills, and it glitters in warm sunshine in the day. It's about three hours south of Tokyo by train, and it lies in a kind of steep horseshoe of land where the mountains meet the bay.

There are so many inns and hotels in Atami that one wonders if anyone here lives in a private dwelling. The streets are filled with souvenir shops. There are innumerable bars and cabarets. There's always an air of gaiety and it's a rare night when you fail to meet celebrants full of sakè clopping through the streets on *geta* (supplied, along with their kimono-like robes by their hotels),

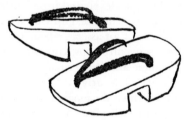

their voices raised in song. There's a huge corps of geisha who make the nightly rounds.

Atami is a hot spring town. It lies in the middle of the tangerine country, and because the mountain range to the west keeps out the prevailing wind, the climate is mild even in the dead of winter. The tangerines are sweet and delicious, and sold everywhere.

ito   Ito is a little further south than Atami. The two cities are similar, with Ito perhaps a little quieter and a little more genuine in atmosphere. It's a favorite resort for Japanese honeymoon couples. Near Ito is the famed Kawana golf course, one of the finest seaside courses in the world. If you make phone reservations at the Kawana Hotel you may, as guest, play the course. Prices are fairly high, but not unreasonable, and the service and accommodations are excellent. There are two other public golf courses in the area and both are a challenge to the duffer who might do well to bring, instead of a caddy cart, a trained mountain goat.

shimoda   This magnificent spot is another two hours by bus or car from Ito. It can't be reached by train. At present the highway is rather rough gravel for about half the distance, but then becomes excellent three-lane blacktop for the rest of the way. It is busily being completed.

Shimoda is the fishing village where Townsend Harris, the first United States consul, was put ashore in 1854 and forced to live in an old temple for a year before he was granted an audience with the shogun in Tokyo. His adventures are now familiar to casual readers and movie-goers. Each year the town of Shimoda holds a summer festival to celebrate Harris' stay, and it's usually attended by the United States ambassador and units of the U.S. Navy, with capital ships anchoring themselves offshore and sending launches into the harbor to take groups of Shimoda's citizens aboard for a tour of the ships.

You will have a quiet time in Shimoda, and the best feature of the area is the marvelous stroll you may take along the winding coastline, in and out of the hidden coves and along rocky beaches. There are several strands of purest white sand where you may

swim. The hotels are good and except in festival season will usually
be able to accommodate you without reservations.

You may see the Buddhist temple where Townsend Harris
lived, and look at several of his personal possessions kept there.
The harbor, with its many small fishing boats, some of foreign
registration, is most worthy of the color camera. Both long shots
and close-ups abound.

suwa   And now I want to tell you about one more resort within
striking distance of the Tokyo area, a lovely spot visited
often by Japanese on a holiday, but seldom by tourists and short-
term residents. I have concentrated in this chapter, by the way,
on locations near Tokyo because the greatest number of foreign
tourists or visitors is in this area; I have not made detailed reports
on Kyoto or Nara, both superb places and musts on your list if
you have time, because they're not quite resort towns. And I've
left out such justly famous hot springs as Beppu, on the southern
island of Kyushu, because of its distance from the capital. Those
who live in these areas may find descriptions of the Kanto area
resorts useful when they come to visit the metropolis, as everyone
does, sooner or later.

Now, Suwa is a lake in the mountains of Central Honshu, the
main Japanese island. It is about five hours northwest of Tokyo
by train. There is a road, but I recommend it only for the hardier
and more patient drivers. There are two express trains a day to
the several towns along the lake, and you board them at Tokyo's
Shinjuku Station on the Chuo Line.

Lake Suwa is about two miles wide and four or five miles long.
It lies in a broad valley that reminds you of Switzerland or places
in Southern Colorado. There are three cities along the lake,
Kamisuwa (Upper Suwa), Shimosuwa (Lower Suwa) and Okaya.
The first of these is a pleasure town, filled with inns and hotels.

Here there is also one of the largest public bathhouses in Japan (maybe the largest) and although there are two separate, huge pools, one for men and one for women, I once entered the latter to take photographs without causing any particular stir or embarrassment. On the lakeside at Kamisuwa you can hire various kinds of boats for a tour on the water and among them, for no reason I've yet been able to discover, is a most unexpected and incongruous genuine Venetian gondola.

Shimosuwa, the next train stop, is slightly smaller and quieter. But it too has a number of comfortable inns, and its countryside offers some of the most picturesque strolls in Japan. There are temples, mountainsides, farms, and covered bridges. There is a large municipal swimming pool where you may take a dip in the summer for ten yen (2.78 cents). In the early autumn there is a festival where the lumberjacks carry decorated logs through the streets to the shrine.

Shimosuwa's economy used to depend on silk, but with the coming of nylon many of the mills closed down. You can still see small silk factories, however, scattered throughout the town, and usually the manager will be delighted to have you walk through and see the silk being made from the cocoon. Because the silk mills employ mostly women, the area has a reputation for housewives who wear the pants in their families. The principal industry there now is a large camera factory.

The third lake city, Okaya, is principally a retail and manufacturing town and is not geared for tourists, though in itself it makes an interesting one-day trip. There are also a number of good bus trips from any of these cities to points in the surrounding countryside, some of them taking you on dizzying climbs on the various mountain roads in the vicinity.

Only a few foreign missionaries live in the valley, and you probably won't even see them. Little English is spoken, but you can get along surprisingly well with sign language and a few guide-book phrases. Prices, in general, are half of what they are at the more popular resorts. The baths are filled with hot-spring water.

Since your train trip takes you a little over five hours, this will necessarily be at least an overnight stop, though I recommend several days. After you've seen the "must" resorts, this is a spot I'm sure will delight you. There are, of course, dozens of others like it, usually a little too far from a major city to be visited quickly, but I mention the Suwa Lake area because I've found it most pleasant and, indeed, return there at least once every year.

karuizawa   Karuizawa is three hours north of Tokyo by train. It lies at the foot of an active volcano. It has golf courses and many tennis courts. If all you want to do in Japan is meet foreigners like yourself, go to Karuizawa.

chapter ten

the japanese inn

It's natural to want to go to "the places the tourists never see," and in Japan you may often *think* you've discovered such a spot, but sooner or later, in some favorite out-of-the-way village, you'll be greeted by an urchin crying: "Hiya, Joe!" or, upon crossing some quiet sylvan glade, you'll stumble over a pile of Schlitz beer cans.

But there's also available in Japan an *illusion* of getting away from it all, and of being the first one to do it. This illusion is easy to come by. Simply spend a few days and nights at a *ryokan,* or traditional Japanese inn.

where
to go
Japanese inns are as thick, in these islands, as shrines or pin-ball parlors. You'll find them in the hearts of the big cities, or on mountain tops deep in the hinterland. The best way to select a location for this particular expedition is to examine your own preferences first, and you might make the first choice between mountains and seashore. If you have lots of time you'll want to travel some distance; if not, you'll be able to find a ryokan practically around the corner from wherever you are.

A small warning before we begin. The Japanese inn is strictly for relaxation. If you're an incorrigible leaping extrovert, the larger resorts will be your dish of *ocha*. There you'll find golfing, shopping, dancing, drinking, and other delightful excesses. In such places you'll have available both modern, Western-style hotels and Japanese inns, and with a little knowledge aforehand you can enjoy the fine experience of staying at one of the latter, for in the *ryokan* you'll find the last traces of the old way of life in Japan: the traditional charm and "differentness" fast disappearing as the country becomes more like the rest of the world.

Select your spot then, according to your needs. Tell someone who knows the country exactly what sort of place you require, then ask him to help you uncover a Japanese inn in that location. The English-speaking clerks at the various offices of the Japan Travel Bureau, which has offices in all cities and many towns, understand this problem and can be most helpful. They'll make your reservations. No charge. Hotel clerks and even maids can assist at this stage.

getting
there
Pick a spot that's easy to reach by motor, train, or bus. Try to avoid too many changes of transportation; avoid a long trip unless it's on a major railroad line, such as the run from Tokyo to Osaka. The debilitating effects of

a prolonged, uncomfortable journey can do a lot to spoil your entire holiday. I've found four hours about as much as I can take comfortably—you may be more rugged.

Japanese train and bus travel is sometimes not so comfortable as the kind you may be used to, and except on certain special lounge trains, such as the "Romance Car" from Tokyo to Nikko, the seats are smaller and not quite so soft. There are second and third class seats, with a negligible price difference between them. Take second class; it's worth it. *Ni-to* is the word for second class, pronounced "knee-toe". No such thing as first class, unless you're the emperor or someone close to him.

Trains are apt to be crowded, especially on weekends, and this means that it's a good idea to get to the platform as much as a half hour early so you'll be sure of space. An even better idea is to take a Japanese friend along, one who'll be more at home and less bashful than you. Let him run in with one bag and grab seats for the party. Another trick is to get a Japanese redcap (yes, Japan has them, and they wear red caps) in the waiting room, give him your bags and ask him to go in and get your seat. He'll be allowed on the platform before the gates open, while a packed line of passengers is still forming. His tip? A hundred yen will do if he hasn't much to carry. Two hundred might be better if you burden him with a heavy load. And incidentally, it will be quite acceptable if you want to give him his tip in advance. He won't be embarrassed; on the contrary, he'll be spurred to more glorious effort.

what to take
You won't have to travel quite so heavily as you do in the United States or Europe because you can get your small laundry—underwear, socks, that sort of thing—done for you at the inn. Unless you're going to a posh resort you'll need nothing formal. In the smaller places, the older

and more comfortable your clothes, the better. Japanese people dress rather quietly when traveling, so hibiscus shirts or red bull-fighter pants might make you a trifle conspicuous. Of course if you enjoy being a trifle conspicuous, well, enjoy Japan.

No doubt you'll want to take your favorite toilet articles, any special face creams or tonics you're accustomed to, but the inn itself can usually supply the basics. Disposable toothbrushes, quite sanitary in a paper envelope, are always available, along with soap, toothpaste, and a razor if you ask for it. No shaving cream—don't ask me why. Japanese men rub ordinary soap on their cheeks and often seem content with old blades that wouldn't cut bean curd. If you use an electric razor you might as well leave it at home; there's plenty of *denki,* or electricity, in a Japanese inn, but the outlets are always in the wrong places if, indeed, they exist at all.

Pack a pair of comfortable shoes—sneakers or slip-on types—to use when you get there. The *geta,* or wooden clogs the hotel lays out, will probably be too small or uncomfortable for you. No shoes in the house, naturally, so the easier it is for you to slip in and out of your footwear as you come and go, the less annoying it will be. For the ladies, we recommend flat heels for country roads.

There's one item that may come under the heading of necessities for some of you, and that's coffee. The inn will have coffee, but it will be of the strong espresso type, and usually not very good espresso. It's also an extra expense. The beverage served as a matter of course is hot, green tea. With a little practice you can get to like the stuff, but if you're a coffee fiend take along a jar of powdered soluble coffee. The hotel people will bring you cups and hot water any time you want them.

arrival   If it's a popular resort you're visiting, or if it's a week-end, or a Japanese holiday, make reservations ahead by telephone. Otherwise it's safe just to show up. Get off at the station, find a cab, and tell the driver the name of the hotel—you've written it down, of course. At some of the more popular spas hotel representatives come to the station to meet the train, and often one of these will find you a billet even if you haven't made reservations. At any rate, the cab driver will take you from the station to the inn, and at the door you will be greeted by a stout company of souls—the proprietor, his wife, all the maids, and the handy man. They will all bow and welcome you with a litany, but all you're required to do is smile and say something nice in English.

Shoes off in the vestibule. You will then be given house slippers too small for your feet. They always fall off when you go up polished wooden stairs, but you can ignore them if you wish and proceed in your stockinged feet. (A friend of mine, who wears an artificial leg, solves the problem by thumb-tacking his slipper on.)

You'll now be shown to your room—a typical Japanese room, complete with alcove, hanging scroll, and mat floor. If you wear slippers, you kick them off in the hall just outside the room. No slippers on the mats, please. In some hotels you may be taken to a tiny separate cottage called the *hanare* (hah-nah-ray) which may have its own rest room.

Inn people seem to think upstairs rooms are more desirable and sometimes charge more for them. I personally prefer first-floor rooms that open on the garden. If you're not satisfied with the room you're shown, it's perfectly all right to ask to see another.

the preliminary conference   As soon as you're settled you'll be brought hot tea and probably one or two little pieces of Japanese cake or candy. You now sip your tea and tell the maid of all your special needs. These might include a kettle of hot water at seven a.m. so you can make your powdered coffee. Tell her at what hours you want your meals. Ask her when the bath will be ready. Order beer or highballs, if you're journey-weary. Order any special foods you think you might need.

All these instructions will call for a certain amount of scrambling over the language barrier, and one way to take care of that right at the start is to use baby talk and sign language to indicate you'd like an interpreter. The hotel can usually find someone around who speaks a little English. But that's rather like cheating, and you may find it more fun to play Spartan Rules. A good dodge is to have a Japanese friend, before you start out, write a number of handy phrases on a series of little cards. Flash these as you need

them. You might include: (1) Where is the *benjo* (toilet)? (2) Can you make scrambled eggs? (3) What time does the noisy party next door stop? (4) Bring on the dancing girls. You know the sort of thing I mean.

time to eat   Better straighten out the food situation right now, at this initial conference. The usual system in a Japanese inn calls for a flat rate that includes your room and two meals, breakfast and supper. Lunch is on your own, or, if the hotel brings it, at an extra charge. The Japanese do not make much distinction between morning and evening meals, and the courses are apt to be similar, with the latter perhaps a shade more elaborate. Plenty of food at both, and the dishes keep coming end-lessly. If you like cereal for breakfast you'd better bring your own. There'll be milk and sugar and, in spite of what military visitors may have been told by abnormally cautious briefing officers, the milk is safe and delicious. If you like ham and eggs you'll probably get them, as one of the courses, at the morning meal. Rice will always be served, usually last, so if you like your rice with your other food, better ask for it to be brought early. If you want toast, ask for it. The Japanese word for toast is—toast.

In many places you'll be charged extra if you order food not on the regular meal plan. In some places they'll consider it a simple substitution. Don't get angry if you run into a mix-up here: the average Japanese inn does not deliberately cheat you.

Inns operate on a rather small margin of profit and if they should rustle up a special dish for you without charge it might very well mean a loss to the house. In fancier places a moderate price for one person per night, with two meals, might be two thousand yen or more. In small places, one thousand—even less occasionally.

There is such a tremendous variety of food in Japan that it's hard to tell exactly what to expect. Each hotel is different . . . each locality has its own specialties and seasonal delights. At shore places seafood is fresh and delicious. In the mountains you'll find more lake and river fish, pork, and chicken. Beef, but not too often. You may not like some of the items, but there'll be so much that you can leave them untouched and still fill yourself.

I'm sure you can use chopsticks by now. Even if you're a new-comer you must have gone the Chinese restaurant route back in the states. But if by any chance you can't manipulate *ohashi,* tell the maid. She'll bring knives and forks. In Japanese you say "knife and fork." Just like that.

The maid will come to your room at various times of day and evening (I don't know when she sleeps) to do small services for you.

She'll show you where the bath and rest rooms are, and do your small laundry. It's a good idea to bring your own towels, by the way, and your own toilet paper. Not all of the smaller places supply these items.

the wonderful hot bath The hot bath should be the high point of your stay at a Japanese inn, especially when it's hot-spring water fresh from the mountain. In spas this is piped right into your hotel. You soap and wash outside the bath, which is usually an attractive tiled pool, and all you do is sit in the hot water and soak. Vocalizing is permitted and encouraged. Take a cold beer with you, if you like. Truly, a sybarite's delight.

The water will be much too hot for you at first and the maid will be happy to run some cold water in to cool it. If you're a male don't be embarrassed if she walks right into the room to do this for you. She's not looking at you. At least, not when you could catch her at it.

If you're still on Spartan Rules you may want to get into the steaming stuff as the Japanese do, and in that case here are a couple of tips that might help. Take a wooden bucket beside the pool and slosh yourself first, lightly, around the wrists, ankles, and the nape of the neck. Then let yourself down into the water by sections: legs, mid-body, and chest. Be sure to stop at the neck. Move as little as possible when you first get in. This is important. When you move a limb you feel the heat more. If you remain absolutely still you can stand astonishing temperatures.

As you emerge you will find yourself as red as a lobster. The Japanese, at this point, always dry themselves with a *wet* towel, and I don't know how it works, but it does. You may now slip into the *yukata*—or cotton kimono—the hotel has provided and return to your room. Here you may order a masseuse or a masseur, a most pleasant experience after the bath. In some of the brighter, wickeder spots the massage girl is really a you-know-what, but this is a problem (or pleasure) you'll have to work out for yourself.

And what do you do between baths and exotic meals?

You stroll in the village.

You see the local shrines or natural phenomena.

Admire the garden of the hotel.

Smoke.

Drink beer.

Talk.

Relax.

Take six or seven baths a day.

At night the maid will spread your *futon* on the soft floor of woven reed. They're remarkably comfortable, all except the pillows, which are tiny and hard and filled, I think, with broken granite. You might bring your own small cushion or air pillow.

sayonara   Now you've had your stay at a Japanese inn and you're ready to go home. Ask for the bill (*kanjo*) and it will be brought to your room. A ten percent service charge will usually be added by the hotel. Tipping is not common in Japan, but it is, nevertheless, a pleasant thing to tip your maid if the spirit moves you, or if her service has been particularly good. Five percent of the bill is plenty.

The hotel will make such arrangements as getting your tickets and calling the taxi to take you to the station. On request, and for a small extra charge, they'll pack a few sandwiches for your train lunch. As you depart the whole company will line up outside of the entrance, bow, wave, smile, and say: "Sayonara!"

You'll have had one of the most delightful experiences of your life at a *ryokan,* or Japanese inn.

chapter eleven

mt. fuji—look or climb?

Fuji, the highest mountain in Japan, is reported in older guide books as having an altitude of 12,397 feet, and in newer accounts as only 12,395, which leads me to the theory that someone has recently climbed to the top, chopped off two feet of mountain, and taken it away as a souvenir.

I come by this suspicion with precedent. I used to know a cocktail party dilletante whose consuming passion in life was to climb Mt. Everest, whose official height is 29,002 feet, remove those last two feet of ice and snow, and leave Everest looming forevermore in round-numbered splendor.

Whatever Fuji's true height, it is hands down the loveliest mountain in the world, its nearest rival for purity of conical form being Mt. Cotopaxi (19,613 feet) in Ecuador.

Fuji is one of a chain of volcanoes which starts far to the south in the Marianas, includes many underwater volcanoes, and eventually runs up a ladder of islands to the southeastern corner of Japan. Fuji is a true, active volcano, but temporarily on inactive duty, so to speak. Its last real eruption was on November 22, 1907, and you can still see bits of steam escaping from fissures in its crater. Volcanologists expect no trouble from Fuji in the foreseeable future, though volcanoes relatively nearby, such as Mt. Asama in Karuizawa, only about 150 miles away, erupt with violence often enough. Fuji is what is called a "composite" volcano as distinguished from the "lava dome" type. The latter is formed by slow eruptions from the flanks of the growing mountain, and the lava flow rarely exceeds twenty-five feet in thickness. Fuji, and other composite volcanoes, are a collection of lava fragments exploded from the throat, plus flows of lava from the top, or from side fissures, and this method of growth is what gives them their characteristic conical shape.

If you should walk around the base of Mt. Fuji you would travel 77.8 miles in an almost perfect circle. If, like the vandals I mentioned earlier, you should get an obsession to carry Fuji away, bucket by bucket, you would find yourself transporting 36,375,995 cubic feet of earth. The mountain's longest lava flow, which is on the northeast side, is seventeen miles long and .6 miles wide. The crater at the top is about 590 yards in diameter and 732 feet deep.

As you can see, Fuji is a well-measured mountain. It's not difficult to climb and more than 100,000 people make the ascent each year, though it's a rather exhausting trip. Many climb it for novelty or pleasure, and some Japanese still regard the ordeal as a sacred pilgrimage. Until 1868 women were not allowed to make the ascent. The first foreigner to reach the top was Sir Rutherford Alcock, a British minister to Japan, on July 26, 1860, and there was some resentment of this sacrilege by certain diehard factions, and an even loftier raising of the eyebrows seven years later when another British minister's wife, one Lady Parkes, also made the pilgrimage. Today foreigners are welcome and, one presumes, even encouraged by the owners of the various inns, restaurants, and souvenir shops along the several roads to Fuji's crest.

Climbing season is in July and August, for only in these months can one expect the top to be entirely free from snow. Determined souls may, however, make the climb out of season—at their own risks. Before you insist on pushing ahead in winter, spring, or fall it's well to remember that scores of people, including a number of Americans and Europeans, have lost their lives in storms or avalanches on Fuji's upper slopes even in recent years.

There is a legend to explain nearly every natural phenomenon in Japan, and there's one for Fuji's almost permanent mantle of snow. It seems an ancient god or spirit once came to Fuji and asked for lodgings overnight. Fuji was too busy to accommodate him and made excuses. Peeved, the god put a magic spell on the mountain so that it would be covered with snow most of the year. "That," he said, "will keep *anybody* from visiting you." The curse, we know today, has backfired nicely.

Nor has Fuji escaped the Japanese fondness for proverbs. You can scarcely discuss the mountain with a Japanese friend without hearing him say sooner or later: "We have a saying: 'If you don't climb Fuji once, you're a fool. If you climb it twice, you're twice a fool.'"

It's a long climb.

You approach Fuji by any of several bus and train routes, and at the base you can begin walking or rent a horse to take you up part of the way. The ascent is marked in ten stations, and you may purchase a climbing stick to be branded at each station, showing that you've passed it. At most of the stations there are stone shelter huts and at some, overnight lodgings and meals. If you are new to Japan it will be best to bring your own food, unless you pride yourself on your adventurous palate. A *goriki,* or mountain guide, can be hired at the starting point to carry any load you've decided to take along, and the nature of the burden should not surprise him since the recent ascent of Fuji by a foreigner who handed his goriki a golf bag and drove a ball before him to the top—number of strokes not recorded.

There are six principal trails up the mountain, all named after their starting points. These are Gotemba, Subashiri, Yoshida, Funatsu, Shoji, and Fujinomiya. Their lengths vary from ten to fifteen miles and the time of ascent from seven to nine hours. Descent is usually clocked at two to five hours. The Yoshida, Shoji, and Funatsu routes are the easiest to climb; the Gotemba route is thought to be the best for descent. In the climbing season special buses run a long way up the mountain before leaving you to your straw climbing sandals. These, incidentally, are quite helpful when tied over your shoes, protecting them from the sharp cinders that make up the mountain; they may be purchased at the bases of any of the routes.

The most popular ascent itinerary is to start early in the afternoon, reach the seventh or eighth station before dark, stay overnight in a stone hut, and continue toward the summit in the morning. The reward for this, if the weather is clear, may be a magnificent view of the sunrise from the top of Fuji. By climbing at night you also avoid the hot sun. Once at the top you'll probably want to walk around the crater, and this takes about two hours.

As we've said, the climb is neither difficult nor dangerous in season—true mountain climbers turn up their noses at Fuji. But the trip is equivalent to walking uphill at a steep angle for eight or nine hours, and if this doesn't appeal to you, eschew the whole thing. If you're still determined, start your expedition by putting yourself in the good hands of the Japan Travel Bureau or the people at any major hotel.

And, by the way, while you're mentioning Mt. Fuji in Japan don't call it "Fujiyama." Somehow this has become the foreign designation for the peak, probably because the word "yama" means mountain. In speaking of it, however, Japanese use a different pronunciation for the same character that depicts mountain. They say "san"—Fuji-san. And this is not the same "san" that's usually affixed to a person's name. By now you're no doubt completely confused. To simplify matters let's say that there'll be no objection at all if you keep it in English and simply refer to "Mt. Fuji."

The mountain's name, Fuji, is of ancient origin and even Japanese scholars are at some disagreement as to its exact meaning. Some say it comes from the Ainu word for fire. Fuji has inspired an awful lot of Japanese art, both good and bad, and there are paintings and photographs of the majestic peak everywhere. It's also celebrated in innumerable songs and poems. One of the favorites is a *waka,* or thirty-one syllable poem. (Thirty-one syllables in Japanese, not necessarily in translation.)

Tago no ura yu	From the place called Tago,
Uchiide te mireba	As I stroll there,
Mashiro nizo	Brilliant and white,
Fuji no takane ni	I see Fuji's crest,
Yuki wa furi keru	Covered with snow.

That this perfect mountain arouses emotion is undeniable. I have had occasion to leave Japan several times during my stay here and, departing by ship or plane, I saw Fuji, white, immaculate, against the sky. I was filled with an indescribable melancholy and a curious feeling of homesickness for a land that was not mine. Perhaps, if you stay long enough, Mt. Fuji will come to mean something like this to you, too.

chapter twelve

fabulous tokyo

Tokyo is not Japan, any more than New York is America. But—if you can unravel this now—Tokyo is much more Japan than New York is America. And the grammar book tells me that "unique" cannot be compared, but all I can say is that Tokyo is about the uniquest doggone city in the world.

It's the world's largest in population. It contains more people than Sweden, Canada, or Australia. It suffered perhaps the worst earthquake in history to occur in a civilized area a little over a quarter of a century ago; it was devastated by bombing in World War II; and today you would need an expert guide to find the slightest scars of either of these travails anywhere in the city limits.

Today Tokyo is filled with gleaming new buildings, its streets are choked with the most modern of traffic, at night it blossoms forth as a garden of neon signs, and it is a city where you can find, at any hour around the clock, virtually any improbable thing you might want, from an agreeably nymphomaniacal companion to a matched set of potted palms.

How did it get this way?

There's the mystery. Tokyo is not a beautiful city—not in the sense that Paris and Bangkok and Kyoto are beautiful. Its climate is so-so: as beastly hot as Washington, D.C. in summer and, if you live in a Japanese house, as chill as Lapland or Tierra del Fuego in the winter. When it's neither hot nor cold it's usually raining. Tokyo is not much of a port; most of the ships put in at Yokohama, twenty-five miles south. Its air-terminal facilities are in no way remarkable. It is so crowded that you half expect its dogs to wag their tails up and down instead of sideways. It is—if you wish to live Occidentally—an expensive city. It's noisy. It is a labyrinth if you haven't a guide. To travel by public transportation is an ordeal; to drive is a struggle; to be a pedestrian is to court suicide.

But nearly ten million people live in Tokyo and more keep pouring in at the rate of 400,000 per year. Among these are several thousand foreigners. Most of them love Tokyo. Many of them stay.

Tokyo, I think, is a sort of mistress one acquires and then, without having planned it that way, falls in love with. In many ways she is a bitchy mistress who demands a great deal. But a fascinating one. For some reason you can scarcely walk two blocks in Tokyo without feeling like the central character in a spy melodrama. She is exotic—no question of that. She is very much alive

... full of movement ... full of people going places and doing things. It is impossible to be lazy or bored in Tokyo.

The harlot, Tokyo, is a youthful doxy with an old hag's wisdom. There is always this amalgam of old and new in the air. You may stare at a gleaming display of electronic gadgets—while you hear the twanging of an ancient samisen from a nearby alley. You may watch a modern, earthquake-proof office building going up—and see the workmen scrambling in split-toed shoes on bamboo scaffolding. Step from your air-conditioned hotel and look across a broad avenue at the looming gray walls of the emperor's palace, a feudal rookery little changed in five centuries.

Tokyo officials date the birth of the city April 1, 1457. This was when a poetic general named Ota Dokan built a stronghold called Edo Castle on the site of the present imperial palace. *Edo* is said to derive from a term meaning "mouth of the estuary," and it is on such a low, marshy formation, essentially, that Tokyo lies. The city of Edo made its first big jump in growth when a shogun named Ieyasu Tokugawa made it his headquarters just before the turn of the seventeenth century. His family ruled Japan for the next two and a half centuries, although the nominal capital was at Kyoto where the emperor sat in rather powerless splendor. Edo became the spiritual and cultural center of the nation. At about the time of the American Civil War, or shortly afterward, the Emperor Meiji took the throne and control of the country along with it. He instituted sweeping reforms, opening and modernizing Japan. In 1868 he moved the official capital from Kyoto to this city of Edo and gave the new capital its present name of Tokyo, or Capital of the East.

Today Tokyo covers an area of 501, 920 acres. It is composed of twenty-three wards, nine cities, twenty-five towns, and fourteen villages. A number of small islands stringing southward into the Pacific are also under the control of Tokyo's Metropolitan Government. And its chief executive ranks not as a mayor, but as a full-fledged governor, the equal of all other prefectural heads throughout Japan.

There are three elements in Tokyo's government: the governor, the assembly, and the administrative commissions. The governor is elected every four years. To vote, you have to be at least twenty years old, and to be governor, at least thirty. You can be elected to the assembly if you're twenty-five. The fixed number of assemblymen is 120, and the body elects its own president and vice-president. Assemblymen also hold their jobs for four years. They meet four times a year, in February, June, September, and December. The assembly enacts, amends, or repeals ordinances, decides on the budget and taxes. The administrative commissions do much of the day-to-day work in governing, and their titles indicate their functions: Electoral, Inspection, Education, Public Safety, and Civil Service.

Wonderful, sprawling Tokyo is just about everything a city can be—from an industrial center to a tourist trap. Most of its industry is what might be called "light," though some steel manufacturing, shipbuilding, and the production of rolling stock goes on within the city limits. The chief products are precision instruments, optical apparatus, medical implements, electronic devices, textiles, leather and rubber goods, bicycles, sewing machines, toys, and foodstuffs. These things are, for the most part, produced by medium-sized companies. The Bureau of Economic Affairs considers this rather a fine state of economic affairs and encourages smaller establishments with suggestions to management and even loans of machinery, presumably to bring them up to the medium-size level.

Tokyo is also a fishing and agricultural city. The fishing industry has three major branches: the production of edible seaweed and shellfish in shallow waters; the cultivation of fresh-water fish, such as trout and carp, and finally, deep-sea fishing in the bay and ocean waters to the south. Annually, 375,000 tons of shellfish are produced. As for agriculture, there are 346,000 farmers in the Tokyo area who, though their numbers are small, supply most of the fresh vegetables for the metropolis. There is also a small dairy industry.

Foodstuffs are wholesale, under the aegis of the Tokyo Metropolitan Government, through a central market and its several branches where thirty-three wholesale companies, 2,974 brokers and 35,000 retailers do business. Meat is slaughtered in a slaughterhouse operated by the city. In recent years, however, there has been a growing demand for meat among Tokyo's citizens and now this slaughterhouse can provide only about fifty percent of the meat needed. The rest comes in from other districts or is imported from abroad, with Australia and New Zealand acting as large suppliers.

Tokyo has innumerable parks, many of them the former gardens of feudal lords. Some, like the Meiji Outer Gardens or Ueno Park, are quite large, others are mere hidden glades and dells to house tiny shrines. Ueno Park boasts the largest zoo in Japan. There is another zoo at Tama Park, thirty kilometers south and west of the Tokyo Station, which is considered the city's center. There are seven public cemeteries and ten crematoria. Cremation is encouraged because of the lack of space for burial. And most corpses, for the same reason, are buried standing.

The quick have their own problems of space and crowding. About half of Tokyo's houses were destroyed by bombing during the war, and while many have been replaced by now, the population has overgrown the *lebensraum*. The Tokyo Metropolitan Government itself has built a number of apartment houses that are rented out to those lucky enough to draw the right tickets in a lottery. The rents are low for these apartments—two to four thousand yen a month, or about $5.50 to $11.00. They are, of course, fire- and earthquake-proof, as are the huge office buildings mushrooming in the heart of the city. The height of any building in Japan is limited to thirty-one meters above ground. (about one hundred feet).

In case of fire or earthquake you'll want firemen or policemen. Tokyo has a number of both, and they are highly trained professionals who rank high in the estimation of their colleagues from other parts of the world. Policemen number 24,000, half of them on constant patrol. There are ninety-one police stations, 766 substations, and 450 police boxes. These police boxes are sheds or other shelters posted in most neighborhoods; they usually keep a list of residents of their areas and can be most helpful when one is trying to find a strange address. Most streets are not named in Japanese cities. Houses are numbered not in geographical order, but as they are built. You find a place in Tokyo by section, ward, precinct, block, and then maddening inquiry. The police department uses radio cars, motorcycles, and has the facilities of a modern crime lab. There is also a Water Police Force for harbor duty.

Firemen have a particularly important job in crowded, volatile Tokyo. There are forty-eight fire stations with 138 branches. Equipment consists of 436 pump trucks, thirty ambulances, twenty-one radio cars, eight turntable ladders, three chemical wagons, and eleven fireboats. More than seven thousand firemen are on duty twenty-four hours a day. There are 3,607 fire-alarm boxes in Tokyo. The city is also dotted with a number of fire watchtowers, which come right out of the past. These may be of wood, steel, or concrete, and on their elevated platforms you may see a firewatcher pacing and staring out over the roofs of his area. Fire officials believe that in many cases these towers still provide the most effective means of spotting and reporting fires quickly.

Tokyo's fire department offers the almost perfect expression of the constant old-mingled-with-new theme that recurs throughout the city. All year the firemen operate with the most modern equipment and then on January 6, just after New Year, they drop everything for the ancient and colorful Firemen's New Year Maneuver. It's called *Dezome* and takes place in Tokyo's huge Meiji Park in front of the Emperor Meiji Memorial Gallery. The firemen don the costumes of the Edo period, and perform acrobatic feats on high bamboo ladders held aloft by their confreres.

If fire is a sometime problem in Tokyo, transportation is a daily and nightly headache. At this writing there are 1,172 streetcars, 1,277 buses, and eighty-nine trolley buses in the city. There are two subway lines and more a-building. The streetcars cover 214 kilometers and carry 1.6 million passengers per day. The buses run 741 kilometers and ring up 760,000 fares daily. The trolley buses take care of another 84,000 riders. The total of these commuters is thirty percent of the passengers who daily move in and out of the downtown area. The other seventy percent use taxis, private cars, motorbikes, bicycles, and shoe leather.

When you hear talk of city planning in Tokyo you will often catch the phrase " green belt " cropping up in the conversation. This is part of the plan to keep Tokyo from stifling itself with growth. The city is now divided into three areas, like the bullseye and next two circles of a target. These are (1) the inner urban area; (2) the green belt area; and (3) the peripheral area. The inner urban area is the main part of Tokyo, within about fifteen kilometers of Tokyo Station. Here building will be carefully controlled and structures made as multi-storied and fireproof as possible. The green belt is a ring to prevent further sprawl, and this is about ten kilometers wide. It will be kept more or less as a rural area, with farms and scenic spots preserved as much as possible. The peripheral area begins about twenty-five kilometers from the center. Here satellite towns will be redeveloped to ab-sorb the population and industry flowing into Tokyo. This plan is necessary because the maximum population that Tokyo can comfortably contain is estimated to be 11.6 million, while, at the present rate, the population by 1967 threatens to reach 14.3 million.

And so Tokyo is big, busy, and fascinating. In twenty-four hours in Tokyo you can lunch with Frenchmen, Indians, Russians, or hooded Arabs, attend traditional Kabuki and, around the corner, take in the latest Hollywood screen spectacle, dine on finest European cuisine, visit a fabulous modern night club, and have a midnight snack of raw fish or chicken liver shish-kebabs in some back alley. You can retire in either an up-to-date hotel room or at a country inn with an artificial waterfall gurgling in the garden just outside the sliding doors. The next morning you can go sightseeing in a rubberneck bus or a pedicab. There used to be fabulous red-light districts, but now that prostitution has been outlawed these no longer exist. But although outlawed, the practice has hardly been abolished. In many bars and cabarets quick, easy, and financially reasonable arrangements may be made. And here again the old mingles with the new for, accord-ing to your preference, you can find your companion in either the latest Paris frock or in traditional kimono.

No, Tokyo is not entirely Japan, but in this city alone there's so much to see and so much to do that it would be understandable if you never managed to get away from it and take in the rest of the country.

chapter thirteen

festivals out the gazoo[*]

You don't have to look for festivals in Japan—they find you.
Not a day goes by in which someone, somewhere, isn't celebrating

* Gazoo=*In copious quantity*. "I've got yen out the gazoo." Etymology
doubtful. Perhaps from "kazoo," a comb-and-tissue-paper instrument often
played in combat areas, and conceivably suggestive of a horn of plenty.

something or other, usually in costume, usually with noise, and invariably in a brilliantly decorated setting. In this chapter we can cover only a few major festivals spread throughout the year so that no matter what season greets you when you come to Japan you should be able to take in one of these *omatsuri*. And where you find yourself, geographically, should make little difference. Cities, towns, neighborhoods, all have their own special festivals, most of them commemorating some event, though you get the feeling that the celebration-loving Japanese really don't need much of an excuse to put on a show.

The ritual of a festival differs from place to place, but generally speaking they're apt to center around the local shrine and to feature singing, dancing, and parades. A typical activity is the carrying of a portable shrine through the streets. The word "portable" here is a euphemism. Often it takes fifty husky men to tote this sacred repository, and to make things even more difficult the spirit within the shrine gets restless at a time like this, causing the entire device to buck and sunfish like a Wyoming bronc. You may think it's only the bearers shaking it, but it's really the *kami* inside.

Let's look at the big festivals one by one and in calendar order.

the new year　　This is the greatest day of the year, comparable to Christmas in our own part of the world, though in late years the Japanese have taken to celebrating Christmas, too—in a rather secular fashion.

On New Year's Eve everything stops and stays stopped for a week. All debts are supposed to be paid by now. Children born in the past year now officially begin their second year of life. Even if they are born a day or two before New Year they are regarded as two years old under the old system, though this is now being replaced by the Western method of reckoning. On New Year's

Eve the whole nation seems to be drawing a deep breath to ready itself for the plunge into the year to come.

Westerners make a cliché of the "oppositeness" of the Orient, but often the notion is true enough, and in a sense it applies to the mid-winter holiday season. We drink and carouse on New Year's Eve. This is more of a family holiday in Japan. Most Japanese now do their drinking and carousing on Christmas.

New Year's Eve is called *Omisoka,* or Great Last Day, and it's a solemn, not a gay event. Late in the evening there's usually a quiet party in the home. Relatives who haven't seen each other all year may get together at this time, sometimes traveling long distances to do so. As you might expect, such reunions promptly lead to feasting, and for this there are special, traditional foods.

Invariably New Year's repasts feature a Japanese buckwheat noodle called *toshi-koshi soba,* whose long noodleshape signifies extended life. Most delicious, by the way. There is also a kind of heavy rice dumpling called *mochi,* which is made by pounding cooked rice into a gooey paste, then forming this into balls. Many Japanese houses have a kind of large wooden mortar in the yard, perhaps made from an upright tree trunk, in which mochi is pounded on the afternoon of Omisoka. Two or three men take long-handled wooden mallets and have a rare old time pounding and kneading the stuff in an intricate rhythm, swinging the doughty mauls and barely missing each other's heads and fingers. For the Japanese, a close call seems to add spice to any occasion. There are even expert teams of mochi pounders who put on special shows at shrines, in theaters, and on TV, and some of these performances are breathtaking. The finished product—mochi—hefts and tastes like a bride's first biscuit, except that it's larger and, I suspect, even less digestible. Apparently, however, you can acquire a taste for the stuff.

If you eat mochi, you probably won't be asleep by midnight,

and this gives you a chance to hear the tolling of the bells. At the stroke of the New Year all Buddhist temples ring their gongs 108 times. The choice of that particular number lies in a complicated Buddhist formula we needn't examine here: enough to say that the sound of the bells chases away all worries and evils.

On New Year's morning, at daybreak, the shrines are crowded —jam-packed. This is quite a spectacle, if you can get out early enough to see it. This is also when the drinking starts and a great many of the pilgrims will be already well potted. From the first to the third of January, offices, schools, banks, shops, and most other places are closed. The celebration lasts for seven days, a period called *Matsu-no-uchi*.

During Matsu-no-uchi it's customary to decorate your house. First, a pair of small pine trees at the front door. In back of each tree, three stems of bamboo. Across the top of the gate or entrance, a rope is stretched and hung with bits of straw or strips of white paper. It's a kind of taboo rope and, in a sense, puts your house off limits to evil spirits.

Within the house you may find such decorations as fern leaves, oranges, or small papier-mâché lobsters. All these decorations have their own meanings. Let's go back to the pine tree for a moment. This is evergreen and thus denotes long life. The bamboo stems, because of their straightness, stand for constancy and virtue. The fern, with its many fronds, suggests an expanding good fortune in the coming year. The orange is used as a symbol because of a pun in the Japanese language. The old word for orange is *"dai-dai"* and this may also mean, "from generation to generation." The lobster, because of its curved back, suggests old age.

Now, on the second day of the season—January 2—the Imperial Palace in Tokyo is open to public visit. People come from far and wide and stream into the palace grounds to offer their congratulations to the emperor between 9:00 a.m. and 3:00 p.m. The emperor, at this time, also makes a personal appearance. In these seven days following the New Year one relaxes at home, attends theaters, night clubs, or restaurants, and makes courtesy calls on friends or business acquaintances. Gifts are often exchanged. And so it is that the Japanese, who love a festival, begin the year with the biggest one of all.

setsubun and bean throwing

If you have secret impulses to scatter things about, *Setsubun* is the festival for you. This is the day when you can throw handfuls of beans all around the house. Let's explain that.

Early in February, usually around the third, there comes a day on which winter is supposed to end and spring begin. This is Setsubun which means, literally, "change of season"—and it's a good excuse for another festival. There may be snow on the ground or weeks of icy weather ahead, but according to tradition winter is finished, and the event is observed with an ancient ceremony that came from Japan to China in the eighth century A.D.

During the evening of Setsubun you're likely to hear someone in the neighborhood crying out: *"Fuku-wa uchi! Oni-wa soto!"*— "Good luck, come in! Devil go out!" And as this cry is uttered, small beans are scattered in each room of the house. They're dried soy beans, available at ordinary shops, and they're carried in a sort of measuring box by the master of the house who, to perform this ritual, will usually don traditional Japanese attire. He tosses handfuls of beans in certain lucky directions, and then he goes through all the rooms and closets, sprinkling each place liberally.

"Fuku-wa uchi!" he cries. *"Oni-wa soto!"*

Why beans? There's a legend—wouldn't you know it! Seems

that during the reign of Uda, 59th emperor of Japan, the Devil lived in a cave. He used to come out at night and upset the neighborhood. The emperor asked seven wise men to put a stop to this mischief and they came up with the formula of throwing parched beans into the cave. Just how this got rid of the demon isn't made clear, but apparently it worked, and today the same ceremony has the same effect.

After the beans are thrown some of them are kept. The belief is that if you eat three of these beans, the first time you hear thunder in the ensuing year you'll never be touched by a thunderbolt, at least until the next Setsubun rolls around. And the beans have other mysterious powers. For instance, if you're a man, and your age is twenty-five or forty-two, you're in an unlucky period. For women the danger years are nineteen and thirty-three. These superstitions are based on certain puns in the Japanese language. Forty-two, for example, can be said *shi-ni*—"four-two." But the word *shini* means "death." So, if you are at an unlucky age, the thing to do is pick up a number of beans corresponding to your age, wrap them in a white paper with a few small coins, and toss them away at the nearest crossroads. That's guaranteed to foil the demons for some time to come.

Two other special charms used in Setsubun seem to me to have a most practical way of keeping demons off. One is a prickly holly branch, the other a dried herring. Hang both over your front door. The prickly branch is likely to ward off the demons by its thorns, but just in case it doesn't, there's the odor of that dried herring to really keep them away.

Setsubun comes in for big public celebrations, too, usually at shrines. At each place there will be a sort of guest appearance by a famous actor, wrestler, or other public figure, who takes a ceremonial part called *Toshi-otoko*. This means, roughly, "Man of the Year." He and the shrine or temple priests will be dressed in ancient costumes and things will begin when the Man of the Year tosses beans out to the crowd. If you catch a few, you can consider yourself quite lucky. Later, an elaborate pageant usually takes place.

A little inquiry on any given year will tell you when Setsubun will be observed and in what shrines and temples. Worth seeing. If you like, bring your own beans.

hina matsuri— the doll festival Japan is a male's country and the big holiday for children is "Boys' Day." There is a girls' day, however. This is *Hina Matsuri,* the Doll Festival, which falls on March 3. *Matsuri* is festival. *Hina,* in one sense, means "baby bird," but it can also indicate a small model or a doll.

Hina Matsuri is the day when little girls display their favorite dolls, and, if they've been good little girls, receive a few new dolls as gifts. The dolls, old and new, are carefully arranged on a set of step-back shelves in the guest room, friends are called in to admire them, and the young ladies sit before the display and eat candies or other delicacies. They dress in their best, brightly flowered kimono. The dolls, too, are elaborately decked out. Heads and hands are usually made of clay or porcelain, but the costumes are of real fabric and this is sometimes precious material. In the few weeks preceding the festival, shops are full of these dolls, and one favorite arrangement is to show them as an old-fashioned Japanese court, the emperor and empress on top, other ranks below.

While admiring their dolls the girls drink something called *shirozake,* which looks like milk, but is really sakè, or a special white rice wine.

Hina Matsuri is not a school holiday, but rather a three- or four-day season that begins on March 3. At this time of year it's a nice thing to send a doll to a new baby girl as a present. Such a doll was originally a superstitious charm to ward off evil and in some remote areas of Japan people still throw these *hina-ningyo* into the river as a protective ritual. This leaves you with the uneasy suspicion that once upon a time it may have been the little girls themselves who were thus dispensed with. Happily, these are modern times. . . .

boys' day The month of May comes into Japan with flowers—and with fish. The weather is usually rainy but comfortable, and as April fades away, huge streaming paper or cloth fish appear on high poles all over the landscape. These are *koi-nobori,* or carp. They're the symbol of Boys' Day, May 5, because the carp has the power to fight its way upstream when the current is swift and thus, because of its determination to overcome obstacles, is regarded as a fitting example for growing boys. These streaming aerial carp are anywhere from one to ten feet long. Usually you'll see several on a pole, one for each boy in the family, the longest fish for the eldest boy, and so on.

Officially, Boys' Day is now called Children's Day, and is supposed to honor both boys and girls, but most people think of it as Boy's Day. And where the girls trot out their dolls on Hina Matsuri, it's toy soldiers that are displayed on May 5. You'll find images of feudal generals and warriors, toy swords, armor, helmets, banners, drums—all the things boys usually like.

I don't know of any traditional sakè drinking on this holiday, however. Here, the girls have the edge on the boys.

tanabata-
the star
festival

In a recent motion picture about Japan the hero and heroine make love on a mossy bank while fireworks burst in the air behind them. "It's Tanabata," says the heroine—and the rest of it is unexplained. Possibly some of the original dialogue fell on the cutting-room floor, but at any rate this section is for those who have always wondered what in blazes that heroine was talking about.

Tanabata, like most other festivals, goes back to a legend. There was a lovely princess—name of Shokujo—who lived in the sky and had nothing to do all day but weave suits for her father, who was monarch of the heavens. One day a handsome herdboy, Kengyo, came along driving his cattle. The two young people glanced at each other and fell in love. The king was against the match; how could a mere celestial cowboy support a princess? The king forbade them to meet, but they began to see each other secretly, anyway. The lovely Shokujo, in love and full of dreams, began to neglect her weaving and the king's garments began to fit badly, (She was surely the ancestress of present-day tailors and dressmakers in Japan.) This made him suspicious and he discovered the secret meetings. At first he said the lovers could never meet again, but Shokujo pleaded until he relented to a degree. He said they'd be able to meet only once a year, on the seventh day of the seventh month.

This, of course, is the date of the Tanabata Festival—July 7.

The first year rolled around and the princess and herdboy each came to the trysting place, which was on a large river—the Milky Way. They were on opposite banks, and the river was too wide for either to cross. The princess began to weep, and suddenly a flock of magpies came along and made a bridge of their out-stretched wings. The lovers met and were reunited.

In areas of Japan where old-fashioned marriage arrangements are still observed, young men and women seldom have a chance to be alone together, but on Tanabata, July 7, the restriction is lifted. The legend goes on to say that if the sky is cloudy on that night the celestial lovers are unable to meet, but a mere overcast is usually no deterrent to mere earthbound couples.

In spite of this festival's romantic background it's usually ob-served more as a family affair, with bamboo trees set in the house and yard for the children and decorated, rather like Christmas trees, with gaudy bits of paper, glass, and plastic. The star motif prevails. Sweet rice dumplings and other special foods are eaten in the home. The shopping areas, for several days pre-ceding Tanabata, are decorated with appropriate doo-dads.

Many neighborhoods sponsor firework displays on the evening of Tanabata, though in Tokyo the huge traditional firework shows come somewhat later in the month, usually around the third weekend of July.

And these are essentially the facts about Tanabata that didn't get into the movie I was talking about.

obon—the welcoming of the ghosts Pronounce it exactly as though you were say-ing: "Oh, bone!" The "O" part is honorific and usually translated as "honorable," which is a rather flavorless way to do it, but so far no better English word has been found. *Bon* might be translated as "soul" or "spirit."

And Obon, to the Western mind, is a curious festival. The whole idea, when the middle of July comes along, is to invite the ghosts of the dead to visit you. Nothing mournful or spooky about it, however—it's always quite a happy occasion.

The climax of a Bon celebration is usually an outdoor community dance on a summer evening. A huge tower or high platform is often erected in open squares, beaches, woodland glades, or other gathering places. The people of the neighborhood dress in *yukata*—cotton summer kimono—and dance in a circle around the pylon. In the old days there was always a small, traditional Japanese orchestra on the platform to supply the music; in these times it's more apt to be a turntable and loudspeaker system. (You might even say a *very loud* speaker system—the Japanese are infatuated with sound amplification, and apparently unable to exercise restraint in its use.) A dance leader, the counterpart of the American square-dance caller, directs the steps and movements with his microphone.

During the Bon season Japanese homes make special preparations for the visiting ghosts, who are usually the spirits of dead relatives and loved ones. A kind of hemp incense is often burned in the vestibule as a welcome fire. Lanterns are hung on doorways or in gardens. Symbolic transportation is provided—perhaps a toy horse made with a cucumber and toothpicks. Food is laid out in front of the family altar, or in some other place of honor.

At many seaside and riverside locations a lantern festival is held in connection with Obon, and lanterns on small toy boats or rafts are set adrift after an appropriate ceremony. These are the dead souls returning, via the sea, to the nether world.

All of this is accompanied by feasting, drinking, and merrymaking, which seems to me, like the Irish wake, a most sensible way to honor the dead, who are doubtless as saddened by gloom as we.

shichi-go-san— the 7-5-3 festival

For fairly obscure reasons children seven, five, and three years old are especially honored in Japan on November 15 each year. In these particular years the children usually receive certain articles of clothing for the first time. A girl of three gets her first hairdress; a boy of five his first *hakama,* or pleated skirt; and a seven-year-old girl her first obi.

The big thing to do on *Shichi-Go-San* (literally 7-5-3) is to take the youngsters to a shrine, usually in the morning. Foreigners often station themselves at any of the major shrines on that date, armed with a camera and plenty of color film. Japanese children have wonderful doll-like faces with bangs like painted brush-strokes on their foreheads, and under them big, licorice eyes.

The children enjoy the outing, not only because they get plenty of special attention, but because of the refreshments and small presents they receive at the shrine. There may be long envelopes filled with candy and printed with good-luck symbols. Boys may receive a small model of Kintoki, who is a kind of young Hercules, and who is said to have once wrestled a bear to a finish. He's often shown riding that bear. Another favorite doll is Daruma, a round figure with a weighted bottom. No matter how often you knock him down he pops upright again. Perhaps young Taro will be given a toy hammer that is supposed to act, when struck, as Aladdin's lamp did when rubbed.

The symbols on the candy envelopes all have to do with long life and prosperity. You'll find the tortoise and the crane—both reputedly highly gerontic creatures; also the pine and bamboo, which remain ever green; the plum, which is the first blossom to appear in spring, often when the snow is still upon the branches, and therefore signifies vigor. And there's apt to be an old couple from a famous story of the Noh theater, a man and wife named Jo and Uba, who stand for long life coupled with happiness.

Parents and youngsters both will undoubtedly be most obliging if you want to take pictures. Don't be bashful. Learn this useful phrase: *"Shashin-wo tottemo ii desuka?"* "May I take your picture?"

Get a Japanese friend to pronounce it for you and learn it as a little song.

tori-no-ichi— the rake fair   This festival is for the birds. At least its name, literally translated, means "Bird Fair." It comes in November on a certain day whose zodiacal sign corresponds with the sign of the bird. Since this day varies from year to year, you'll have to ask around or consult one of Japan's fine English-language newspapers to learn the exact date.

With the usual amiable absence of logic applied to these matters—a habit the Japanese seem to share with their island-dwelling cousins, the British—the Bird Fair has very little to do with birds. It's really concerned with rakes. Not the kind who progress, but the kind that are garden implements. Rakes are the symbol of this festival, because they also symbolize the gathering-in of wealth and this, in a sense, is a businessman's festival.

On the day of Tori-no-ichi many of the shrines in Japan are surrounded by dozens of little booths or lean-tos in which all manner of goods are sold. Bargaining is not common in Japan, but on this day bargaining is both expected and enjoyed. A rake is one item you might wish to buy as a souvenir. They come in all sizes, from a few inches to several feet long. Some are of plain bamboo, some are elaborately decorated. Upon them you may find such lucky symbols as a bale of rice (for plenty), a ledger book (for profits), gold pieces, and the omnipresent crane and tortoise, or the ubiquitous septet of the lucky gods. There may be a certain old couple: a grandfather with a rake to collect all good things, a grandma with a broom to sweep all bad things away.

As for the bargaining, there's a formula. Figure the object to be worth roughly half of the asking price. Make your first offer half of what the merchandise is worth. Proceed, in jocular steps (never lose your temper as in Mediterranean bargaining), from these two extremes to the final and fair cost.

If you're a good unreconstructed economic royalist and a sharp horsetrader, the Festival of the Birds is for you.

These are the big festivals but, as we said, there are dozens more. The Japanese are a most sociable folk and will usually drop everything if there's a festival in sight. They welcome you as guests at these affairs—in fact they're usually eager to show and explain everything to you. Whatever time of year you arrive, you should be able to find a festival going on somewhere. By all means attend. It's in the festivals that the best part of the old spirit of Japan still survives.

things

chapter fourteen

for stout hearts and strong stomachs—japanese food

A friend of mine, recently arrived from the United States, speaks of the boom there in things Japanese and tells me that you may now purchase a number of Oriental delicacies in certain big American department stores. He attended one affair where the host had laid in a supply of canned roasted grasshoppers from Japan. These he substituted, at about the fourth round, for olives in the martinis. The effect, my friend reports, was devastating. He still looks a little bit dazed whenever he recalls the incident.

Notions of what is and what isn't edible still form one of the broadest areas of difference between East and West. And it is in this field that true tolerance, along with admirable discipline of the palate, may be exercised.

I am going to discuss some of the exotic items the Japanese regard as perfectly good food, but before I do I would like to point out that on this globe of ours you can still find societies where such things as beef, pork, ice creams, and tomatoes are considered revolting fare. Indeed, when America's first consul, Townsend Harris, came to Japan in the 1850's, his hosts were shocked at his apparent need for the nauseating white liquid, from the udder of a cow, known as *milk*.

But let us not plunge too suddenly into this business of unaccustomed foods. Let's begin with a familiar item that seldom offends Western taste buds.

sukiyaki Ninety-nine out of a hundred visitors to Japan have sampled *sukiyaki* elsewhere, and while today it may indeed be described as a Japanese dish, it is one of fairly recent origin, for until about a hundred years ago beef was not eaten in Japan, and beef is the mainstay of sukiyaki. (You can also get chicken or pork sukiyaki, but these are variations.)

The dish was invented during the last century under the rather wistful assumption that it was not an Oriental but a Western recipe. Probably it was inspired by the various beef stews foreigners were known to admire. It also seems to resemble, in some respects, the Chinese method of serving beef and vegetables. Whatever the true origin, the dish became popular with the Japanese themselves and before long they discovered, with some surprise, that it was regarded as a native preparation. It is truly delicious. If you're one of the rare few who have never sampled sukiyaki, a description is in order. It's cooked on the table, before you, in a shallow skillet over a gas or charcoal fire. This preparation at the table before your eyes is the point of the whole affair, for it doesn't taste nearly so good if cooked in the kitchen and brought out ready to eat.

I might as well give you the recipe the average Japanese housewife uses to make sukiyaki. I can't give you quantities and measurements, however, for it simply isn't done that way. The reason for this will be clear in a moment.

First, the ingredients:

1. A chunk of beef fat.
2. Some finely sliced tender beef.
3. A few stalks of *onegi,* Japanese leeks. Onions will do.
4. A few mushrooms. Fresh better than canned.
5. Greens, such as chrysanthemum leaves. Spinach works.
6. A quantity of something called *shirataki.* It's a kind of vermicelli made out of a tapioca-like substance. Comes fresh or in cans.
7. A square or two of *tofu,* a gummy white soybean curd.
8. Soy sauce. Must be real Japanese soy sauce.
9. A few spoonfuls of sugar.
10. About one-fourth cup of sakè.
11. A little water for thinning.

Quantities depend on how many people you wish to serve. You might figure on about half a pound of beef per person. It must be top grade, tender meat. In Japan you can get it already sliced for sukiyaki; elsewhere you'll probably have to order something at least as good as filet mignon, and have the butcher put it on his slicer and cut it as fine as sandwich ham or pastrami.

Now you don't make your *sukiyaki* all at once, but a skilletful at a time, as your guests are eating. You can use any round, shallow, iron pan—a regular frying skillet will do. In Japanese hardware shops you can buy either a small charcoal burner for the table, or gas plates which you can connect by hose to an outlet, if there's one available. The charcoal burners are cheap and nice to take home. Here's how you proceed:

1. Lay out raw ingredients on a separate plate.

2. Get the skillet good and hot, then rub it thoroughly with the beef fat until it is well greased.
3. Put in enough beef to cover the skillet bottom.
4. Put the onegi, or onions, in.
5. Brown beef and onions well. The beef should be seared rather quickly to keep the juices from escaping.
6. Add mushrooms, greens, shirataki, and tofu. Any quantity —it's up to your feeling. Let these get slightly brown, too.
7. Now put in about one cup of soy sauce.
8. Sprinkle perhaps three teaspoons of sugar over everything.
9. Add about one-fourth cup of sakè.
10. Taste the juicy stock now formed, and adjust with soy sauce or sugar according to saltiness or sweetness you desire.
11. Let everything simmer over a low flame. As the skillet is emptied add more meat, vegetables, etc., in any order or quantity to keep it going. Thin the sauce with water when necessary.
12. Serve in small individual dishes with a bowl of hot rice on the side. Sakè, warmed and in thimble-sized cups, is the ideal drink with this meal.

And one more item to make it all completely authentic—pronounce the name of this dish "skee-yah-kee."

sushi Even more characteristically Japanese is the snack or canapé dish known as *sushi*. Basically sushi consists of raw seafood placed on little oblong patties of cold rice. The seafood is no rawer than the clams or oysters you've probably eaten many times in the Western world.

Sushi shops are all over in Japan; there's not a neighborhood without one. They're built to resemble old-style Japanese cottages and in one you'll find several tables and a bar-like counter. You can sit at the table and order a plate of mixed sushi, known as *ichi-nin-mae* or "in front of one person." If you know what you like best, you can sit at the counter and order the bits individually as the mood strikes you.

Each sushi piece is enough for about two big bites. The rice block underneath is treated with weak vinegar to make it hold together. A slice of seafood is laid atop the block. A small quantity of hot, green Japanese horseradish known as *wasabi* is daubed on the underside of the seafood. You will have a little dish of soy sauce at your side, and if you're a true connoisseur, you will hold the canapé upside down, and dip the seafood, not the rice, into the sauce. You will also be served steaming hot tea known to sushi fans by a special word: *agari*.

At the counter various ingredients are laid out before you, usually in a glass-topped refrigerated case. Most popular with foreigners is the meat of tuna, called *maguro*. Regular tuna is brick red and has a fine, beefy taste; a more special kind is paler, richer, oilier, and called *toro*. There will usually be some kind of white fish meat, perhaps *hirame* (flounder); *tara* (bass); or *tai* (sea bream). None of these tastes as strong or fishy as you might imagine—the flavor is really quite delicate. If you happen to prefer that salty seashore taste, however, you might try *kohada,* a silvery speckled fish I believe may be a sort of herring, or *aji,* which is a tiny mackerel. For those with strong bicuspids there will be both *tako* (octopus) and *ika* (squid). Usually you'll find several kinds of shellfish. There is a reddish clam that is eaten raw, and there are often ordinary clams, which are cooked and daubed with a special brown sauce. A fine shop may also add a drop of lime juice to these. You can get slices of abalone, or scallop. For those who don't like *any* kind of seafood there is a gourdlike vegetable called *kampio* which is rolled in a small cylinder of rice and a paper-like seaweed, and also a kind of omelet cut in strips and laid on the rice blocks. Sushi fans will tell you that the quality of the shop can be estimated from this egg canapé, and this is what they will order first when trying out a new place.

Beer is wonderful with sushi, and can be ordered in all shops.

soba   Admittedly, sushi is exotic and you may feel more comfortable beginning your acquaintance with one of Japan's many tasty noodle dishes. These again are served in special shops, although they may also be ordered in many regular restaurants. The generic term for Japanese noodles is *soba,* though strictly speaking soba stands for one particular variety.

The true soba enthusiast prefers his bowl of noodles served from a wandering peddler's cart late at night after a good geisha party or other pleasant diversion. These soba carts have been thinning out in late years and, one reflects with a sigh, may one day disappear altogether from the Japanese scene. They have two wheels, stand a little more than man high, and are covered with a canopy. There's a roof that makes a cart resemble a small cottage. Within the body of the cart there is a receptacle for a charcoal fire and above it a huge well or two in which the food is kept warm. The soba man announces his presence in the streets late at night with a tiny, double-reeded horn known as a *charumera*. He plays a standard tune which is one of the loveliest, most haunting sounds in Japan:

Probably the soba cart is one of the most unsanitary methods of getting your noodles in Japan, but all I can say is that after considerable patronage most of my friends and I are still alive and healthy.

The noodle man and his cart will usually offer only a few kinds of soba, but in a shop you can get almost infinite variations on the basic dish, all of them delicious. Basically, you get noodles in a soup bowl filled with steaming hot brown sauce. There are three kinds of noodles: *soba,* which is a darker buckwheat noodle, somewhat thin; *udon,* a fat white noodle, and *Shina-soba,* Chinese noodle, which is pale yellow and has a permanent wave. The ingredients placed atop the noodles make the different dishes.

You can order your noodles with pork, beef, chicken, or egg. With the meat you will usually have a few pieces of mushroom, bamboo shoot, Japanese leeks, and slices of prepared fish foods that are peculiar to Japan. One of these is a spongy stuff made of fish meat and bone and called *hanpen.* Another is a firm, cheeselike cake of fish product called *kamaboko.* There may also be shrimp dipped in batter and deep-fried. One Shina-soba dish gives you a fair sampling of all these goodies: it's called *go-moku-soba,* or Five Variety Noodles.

hotel and inn food Meals in ordinary Japanese homes are apt to be rather simple and fairly economical, but if you go to a special party at a fancy restaurant, or stay at a Japanese inn, you're likely to have a most exotic banquet placed before you at supper time. In some of the side dishes you'll find various kinds of vegetables, including cabbage and white radish pickled in brine. Tart, but quite tasty. Cooked beef, pork, chicken, and fish will often be served covered with a sweetish gravy or sauce. The Japanese use a great deal of sugar in their cooking, a taste combination, unfortunately, that most Westerners don't prefer; and the Japanese also don't insist that their food be piping hot when it arrives—in fact they often prefer it cold.

At some time during every meal you're bound to get some sort of really delicious cooked fish. The varieties seem endless in Japan. Trout is superb. Flying fish is most delicate and resembles chicken. There is a kind of steak of *buri,* or yellowtail, which tastes like swordfish, but is not nearly as dry. *Sashimi,* or raw fish, is also a standard item: so are tuna, flounder, bass, sea bream, many others. With the slices of sashimi you'll be given a pat of wasabi (the mustard-like green horseradish) and a sprig of herb called *shisonomi.* Draw the buds from this herb by sliding your pinched fingers along it and let them fall into your soy sauce. And a dab of wasabi. Mix. Now pick up the fish slices and with your chopsticks dip them into this dressing before eating.

The hotel or fancy Japanese-style restaurant meal will also often include familiar items. Lobster is small but delicious in Japan. Shrimp or prawn are battered and fried in deep fat—this is called *tempura,* and there are many restaurants specializing in this alone. Frequently pork cutlets, roast chicken, steak, or roast beef will be included as one of the courses. Beef is superb in Japan, and about half the price of U.S. beef. Reputedly the best is Kobe beef, and I have been told for years that the cattle are massaged for several weeks before slaughter to make them tender, though I've been unable to ascertain the real truth of this. At any rate, the beef alone is enough to keep some of us old residents from ever wishing to leave.

The items I've discussed so far are more or less regular foods, and I've saved the really exotic numbers for last. Dessert, if you will. These are fairly uncommon delicacies, but readily available in Japan.

connoisseurs'
items
You might begin with *hachi-no-ko*—bee grubs fried and cooked in sauce. You can get them canned in almost any grocery shop, especially those in big department stores. They taste rather like pecans. Then, of course, there are the grasshoppers we've already mentioned. These are cooked in a soy and sugar sauce so that they're black and shiny. A favorite breakfast food is *tara-no-ko,* the roe of bass, which is tinted red, broiled, and eaten with rice. It's like our shad roe, but not nearly so fishy. Quite salty, however. Japanese salmon eggs resemble good caviar. Often you can get them in a sushi shop, atop a patty of rice and contained by a thin wall of seaweed wrapped around the rice to form a crown. Sushi shops also feature raw, slate-blue sea slug, if you can stand it. In the country, people often prepare various snakes, newts, and lizards as food, but you're not apt to find such fare in restaurants.

Now it's time to tell you of my favorite shocker. I've tried it only once, because of a private vow to taste anything at least once. When the season is right you can go into any good sushi shop and ask for *nama-ebi*. The attendant will select a live shrimp, strip away the carapace and hand you the torso to be eaten, still quivering, on the tongue.

There's one more food that deserves mention because it affords a comment on Japanese character. This is *fugu,* or blowfish. If you've deep-sea fished in the United States, you've caught blowfish and no doubt amused yourself by tickling their stomachs until they puff up to several times their normal size. Their flesh, as a matter of fact, is quite good and is usually eaten raw, in thin, delicate slices. The only difficulty is that the bile of blowfish is a deadly poison, and if so much as a drop is consumed, a man may die in only a few seconds. This, many Japanese friends tell me, provides the real zest of blowfish eating. Men who prepare fugu must do so most carefully to eliminate the poison from the flesh. They serve long apprenticeships and are licensed by the government. In spite of this, several Japanese die each year from fugu. If you like living dangerously, try some.

Whatever your tastes, put aside your gastronomical prejudices in Japan. For when it comes to tolerance and understanding, the stomach is as good a place as any to start.

chapter fifteen

pearls

Going home from Japan without a string of pearls is like leaving Atlantic City without a box of salt-water taffy, or Southern California without an avocado.

Of all the products of this remarkable nation, *shinju,* or pearls, are perhaps the most characteristic, and their excellence can, in a large measure, be traced to a man named Kokichi Mikimoto. Before Mikimoto, pearls, like gold, were where you found them. They were an accident of nature, precious and rare. Real pearl necklaces were reserved for kings and millionaires, and only nature could make a pearl. Mikimoto changed this forever. How he did it is quite a story.

the oyster's tear   "The pearl," an old saying used to go, "is the oyster's tear." This is more poetic than accurate. The pearl is formed in oysters (or other shellfish) when a foreign body or a grain of sand is introduced. It is made of exactly the same substance as the lining of the shell, or mother-of-pearl. First this grain of sand accidentally lodges itself in a weak place in the lining. The lining, as a matter of course, grows over it. In most cases, when this happens, you will merely find a lump in the lining, but when a second accident takes place the lump is dislodged, and it begins to roll about in the shell. The rolling rounds and polishes it. When the pellet assumes its final spherical form we have a true pearl.

That this doesn't happen too often in nature can be seen in a tally made in 1957 at some oyster beds in the Persian Gulf. The crew of one boat opened a week's catch—35,000 pearl oysters. Out of all these, how many pearls? Twenty-one. And of these twenty-one—*only three were good enough to be sold as gems.*

But Japanese pearl raisers, instead of waiting for the rare accident that produces a pearl, control the process from the beginning. That's not so easy as it sounds: there's more to it than simply dropping a grain of sand into an oyster and hoping for the best.

The earliest attempt to produce pearls artificially was made by the Chinese in the twelfth century. We have no really accurate records on these experiments except a few accounts telling us that these man-made pearls were not nearly so fine as the natural gems. Later, the great Swedish botanist, Carolus Linnaeus, also discovered a way to produce cultured pearls, but again with only limited success. Both the early Chinese and Linnaeus used fresh-water mussels rather than oysters—and incidentally it is these creatures that produce pearls raised in the United States.

It's not generally known that there is actually a small U.S. industry in pearl production. American pearls come from fresh water shellfish found in streams and lakes, and they are especially numerous in the Mississippi Valley. The value of mussel fishing in the United States is about three million dollars yearly, with perhaps a third of that amount from the sale of the shells for various uses. Nor are the pearls inferior. When you find a good fresh-water pearl, it usually has exceptionally fine color and beauty and is highly valued, and, like marine pearls, these are most often discovered in distorted or otherwise imperfect shells. But these again are natural pearls—they must be prospected for rather than made.

the first experiments When Kokichi Mikimoto began to look for a way to produce pearls at will, he began by carefully studying all the previous attempts that had been made. He was born in Ise Province, on the south-central coast of Honshu, Japan's main island, in 1858. There was already a minor pearl industry near his home; natural pearls were found there, but were somewhat inferior in quality to pearls from other places.

Mikimoto saw that experiments with mussels had not been too successful, and decided to use the same oysters that produced genuine pearls. He worked tirelessly and in 1896 succeeded in producing what is called a "blister pearl." The name about describes it—an irregular object with blisters on its surface. What Mikimoto had not been able to bring about was the second step in that natural process: the polishing of the pearl by its rolling movement in the shell.

It was 1909 before a man named Nishikawa, who worked for the Japanese Bureau of Fisheries, produced a truly spherical cultured pearl, but at great effort and expense, which precluded his using the process commercially. (A team of American university scientists once actually made a silk purse from a sow's ear, at a cost of about twenty times a good, natural silk purse.) Nishikawa's work, however, contributed greatly to the mounting knowledge of pearl production.

pearls—
at any price
By this time Mikimoto had established a cultivating farm in Ago Bay and there, working under a Dr. Kakichi Mitsukuri, he had learned to produce what might be called "half-pearls"—hemispheres, rather than perfectly round objects. He wasn't, of course, satisfied with this. He continued to work, night and day, against financial odds and cynical enemies.

His labors finally brought forth one key contribution to the science of pearl culture. Previously, everyone had thought that the foreign substance—the grain of sand, for instance—placed in the oyster was the most important factor in getting a pearl to form itself. Mikimoto learned that the real crux of the problem was in something called the "pearl sacs," a kind of bubble formed in the mother-of-pearl lining. Sand wasn't needed. Formation of the pearl could be stimulated by other means—by chloride injections, for example.

In 1913 Mikimoto produced the first really fine cultured pearls. He invented a device called the "culturing cage"—a kind of basket for holding about a hundred pearl oysters as they grow in beds beneath the sea. This allowed the oysters to be hauled to the surface several times a year, and to be cleaned and scraped. Thus, barnacles, seaweed, and certain harmful chemical substances which would ordinarily inhibit or ruin the formation of a pearl could be removed.

Today, in the cultured pearl farms of Japan, more than ten million oysters are cultivated in a year, and three million new ones bred.

The best way to be sure of quality in the pearls you buy in Japan is to go to large, reliable pearl shop. There are always several in the big cities, and the department stores invariably have pearl sections where you can buy with confidence. For those in the U.S. Forces, the exchanges sell good quality pearls at about a ten percent markdown. You can buy a very decent string of pearls in Japan for as little as twenty-five dollars. If you want to pay more you can begin to acquire exquisite sets of perfectly matched pearls that will excite envy anywhere in the world.

Old Kokichi Mikimoto died some years ago, but his descendants still carry on the business of culturing pearls and Japan remains the world leader in this field. Today you cannot distinguish a fine cultured pearl from a natural one.

odd fact   Perhaps you can work this one into a conversation some day. The oyster is peculiar among living creatures. He begins life as a male, goes through several changes, becoming female, then male again, and so on, before he perishes. This intelligence has moved this writer to poesy:

> The poor, unpredictable oysters,
> (Not one of whom gambols or roysters),
> Produce cultured pearls,
> Both as boys and as girls,
> In the quiet of their calcium cloysters.

chapter sixteen

japanese sports

The better sports writers have a way of waxing philosophical, a fact that always seems to escape the lesser sports writers who think a man has to be a slob in order to comment on such physical matters; and so let us begin this dissertation on Japanese sports with a few reflections.

In love and hate, as in negative and positive electricity, there is an attraction of opposites. Love and hate may exist ambivalently in what amounts to a single emotion. And in the list of common opposites we often find the terms Oriental and Occidental. Since they are regarded as antonyms, they reflect an assumption prevalent in the West that Orientals are in most ways diametrically unlike ourselves. This assumption has led to incomprehension, embarrassment, dislike, and, in wartime, downright hatred between peoples of the East and West.

Now I would like to make the proposition that such clashes between two groups are as much the result of *sameness* as of difference. This is a common situation when, for example, husband and wife are too much alike; matched pairs of artists, neurotics, imbeciles, geniuses, sports champions, and so on, are nearly always at each other's throats. And I would like to suggest further that the field of sport shows us how very much like us Westerners the Japanese are, basically. Sport, like the frontier tale, boils human conflict down to its essentials and both symbolizes and dramatizes it with unmistakable clarity.

And the Japanese play at and react to sports exactly as we do; they thrill at a close contest, worship sports heroes, and put great stock in fair play.

The only real difference is in the minor rules and methods of Japanese sport. There is one odd fact to be noted, however. None of the *traditional* Japanese sports, as far as I have been able to discover, involves *team* play. They nearly always pit individual against individual in the moment of the contest, although groups may vie with each other through accumulating points racked up by the individuals. This is rather a curious state of affairs in a nation that so far in history has displayed an almost tribal unity of thought, and it may be that in spite of the homogeneity of the Japanese they have not, until recent times, had a very highly developed sense of social responsibility, substituting for it their intricate pattern of family and institutional obligations. And in this connection it may be significant that the popularity of the imported team sport, baseball, is a thing of modern times.

The fact is, baseball is perhaps Japan's most popular sport these days. Even during World War II it continued as popular as ever—but with one small modification. The *Kempei-tai,* or

Thought Police, decided no English words should be used, and umpires, sports writers, and the like were required to call out the awkward Japanese equivalents for "Strike!" "Ball!" "Home-run!" etc. Usually everyone was quite obedient, but whenever the play became heated they would forget the prescribed terms and revert back to "Strike!" "Ball!" Today, of course, these are perfectly good Japanese words.

But on to purely Japanese sports.

sumo This is the big one.

Sumo wrestling is the sport you hear about before you come to Japan, and the sport you always want to see first when you get here. Unfortunately it's not easy for a foreigner to see a sumo match. Not impossible, but still, not easy. Spectators sit in boxes rented for the season, and these are usually taken up by companies or other big institutions. You can, however, get more distant seats by purchasing tickets, or you might even wangle an invitation from someone who has a box.

In these boxes—which are really just roped-off areas—you squat on mats, Japanese style, nurse the pins and needles in your legs, and munch on goodies and drink sakè. You go for a whole afternoon and see a series of matches beginning with the younger wrestlers and working right up to the leading champions who do their stuff at around 5:00 p.m. If you're a real fan you attend all the days of a tournament, which lasts about two weeks. Tourna-ments are held several times a year, usually in the fall and winter seasons, in the bigger cities. Touring sumo troupes of lesser-known wrestlers often visit the smaller places and perform what amounts to one-night stands.

Sumo is basically wrestling, but what makes it delightful is the tradition and ceremony surrounding it. The sport goes back to the tenth century, and possibly before that. Grand champions today on formal occasions wear huge white ropes about their midriffs because an ancient wrestler named Hajikami once tied a thick rope about his middle and defied any opponent to touch it.

In the ring modern sumo wrestlers wear a sort of combined sash and loincloth of heavy silk, from which hang a number of stiff, knee-length tassels. The tassels often come off during a match and are swept out of the way by the referee. The loincloths themselves often come loose, as a matter of fact, in which case the referee usually stops the bout and makes adjustments before the wrestler finds himself caught with his pants down.

The object of a sumo match is (a) to throw your opponent out

of the ring, or (b) to cause any part of him, other than his feet, to touch the ground. The wrestlers meet in a sand-floored ring about fifteen feet in diameter. They salute each other with traditional gestures and then each takes a handful of salt from a small box near his corner and sprinkles it into the ring in a gesture of purification. They squat and glower at each other brow-to-brow several times, and the suspense mounts. The match will not begin until both men decide to charge forward simultaneously. Often they put this off for long minutes, rising, returning to the salt box, rinsing their mouths with water, posturing, and gesturing all over again. Foreigners often wonder why in blazes they don't begin, but sumo fans know that this preliminary is called *shikiri-naoshi,* and that it can be used by a clever wrestler to secure a psychological advantage over his opponent by making him wait and staring him down.

However, when five minutes have passed the wrestlers must fight, and as the deadline of *"jikan-ippai"* approaches, the fans begin to roar with anticipation. Finally the referee signals a start and the two behemoths charge and clash.

Ordinarily the match lasts only a few minutes, though occasionally two men manage to grip each other's sashes and stymie each other for long periods. There are forty-eight holds and throws by which an opponent may be bested. Some of the more spectacular devices are: Picking up a man and depositing him outside the ring; stepping aside as he charges, and slapping him on the back to send him down; tripping him over an outthrust leg. Often the victor falls with the vanquished, but the rule is that whoever strikes the ground first loses. Such an ending often led to close arguments in older days, but in modern times the TV kinescope usually settles the matter.

As for the wrestlers themselves, they come from all parts of Japan, and from all stations in life. They are not, as some foreigners think, "bred" for size. Size, however, they have. Most modern wrestlers reach around six feet. Many are taller. A wrestler of the 1829's was said to have been seven feet, three inches tall. In the 1920's there was a junior champion who weighed around four hundred pounds. Youths of fourteen or fifteen who seem to be growing large will often be apprenticed to the sport, especially in rural districts.

Sumo is full of ceremony, beginning with a sort of Grand March early in the day when all the wrestlers parade in full and gorgeous costumes, and ending with a bow-twirling ceremony at the conclusion of the matches. This goes back to a wrestler of the late sixteenth century who won a bow for a prize, and it's said this same bow is used in the ring today.

When you begin to sense a few of the rules and start to learn the names of the players, sumo can be as exciting as any sport you've ever watched, and after a few matches it's a mighty jaded fellow who doesn't become a dyed-in-the-wool fan.

judo Judo is another form of Japanese wrestling. And that's really all it is. A great deal of mystery and exotic atmosphere has always surrounded this sport, especially since a version of it was taught to commandoes, marines, and such in World War II, presumably to enable them to defeat any swarms of huge, armed men trying to attack them. On the whole, such a reliance on judo is nonsense.

Judo was not meant to be a 97-pound weakling's secret weapon. True, part of its technique involves overcoming an opponent by cleverly turning his own momentum and strength against him, but if this were the whole story *the little guys would always win and the big guys wouldn't have a chance!*

It's a sport, pure and simple. There are certain holds and techniques which each opponent has a right to use. There are, as in any sport, certain limitations, certain illegal attacks. Those who have a misplaced faith in judo as a secret weapon forget that in a knock-down, drag-out fight the opponent is not going to abide by these rules and limitations. The best that can be said of judo as part of a marine's or an FBI man's equipment is that it keeps him in good physical condition and sharpens his reflexes. But then, so does Greco-Roman wrestling, and so does boxing and so, for that matter, does golf.

On the judo mat, which means under ideal conditions, the wrestlers begin by grasping each other's loose clothing, then they dance around a bit until one can trip, flip, or throw the other. Although it is against the rules to kick or strike a man in certain spots and supposedly knock him out this way, I am told that this sometimes happens in non-sporting situation, but I have never seen it and I have a strong suspicion that it cannot be easily done.

Boxers have been matched against judoists several times. The boxers have always won.

kendo   This is Japanese fencing. It differs from European fencing as the Japanese sword differs from the foil, epée, and saber. The original Japanese *katana* is about four feet long and a formidable weapon indeed. Heavy, single-edged, and razor sharp, it can lop off a man's head with one blow, and often has. The steel is tempered by special craftsmen, usually from old swordmaker families, and since it is not stainless, great care must be taken to keep it from becoming pocked or tarnished. The blade should never be touched with the finger—acids from the skin pollute it. When a Japanese man cleans his sword he puts a folded piece of tissue in his mouth to keep his breath from contaminating the metal.

The swords in *kendo,* however, are bamboo replicas of the real thing. This doesn't mean that they can't hurt when they strike. There's nothing that raises quite the welt that bamboo does. Consequently, kendo fencers wear metal head cages, breastplates, greaves, and gauntlets. The sword handle is fifteen inches and is held with two hands. You swing at the head, trunk, or arms and you may also thrust at the throat. A match consists of two out of three touches.

Officials of the early Occupation after World War II tried to abolish kendo as too warlike in spirit, but as soon as that absurd ban was lifted kendo came back in full force and today is as popular as ever, especially in schools.

There is one form of kendo where top experts give exhibitions with real swords and the skill with which they barely miss each other is breathtaking. Such a contest has all the tension of a good bullfight. A real Japanese sword is supposed to be capable of cutting through a piece of fine silk floating in the air.

archery The bow and arrow have a long tradition in Japan, and in ancient times the inhabitants of these islands were renowned as archers. The Japanese bow is made of bamboo and is seven feet, six inches long. It differs from the Western bow in that its cast is somewhat lopsided; the top portion is longer than the bottom. The technique of shooting is also somewhat different, for the Japanese archer, instead of drawing the arrow notch to his cheek, lifts both bow and arrow slightly as he draws, then brings the feathers slowly down into position near his eye for the release.

One interesting variation on the sport is *yabusame,* or archery from horseback. Exhibitions of this take place at various shrine festivals, usually in the autumn. The most famous is the yabusame event at Kamakura's Hachiman shrine around the middle of each September. You can consult your local papers and weekly guides for the exact date. Archers in medieval costumes gallop full tilt past targets laid along the course and split them with shafts—a most impressive show of skill.

hanetsuki This minor sport hardly belongs with the others, since it's primarily a children's New Year's activity, but it's so typically Japanese that it bears mention here. In a word, *hanetsuki* (pronounced hah-net'-skee) is Japanese badminton. It is played with small wooden paddles and little feathered pellets, usually of lead. The paddles are decorated with samurai faces or other designs and range from cheap toys to elaborate implements used for decoration only and kept in glass cases. These paddles are known as *hagoita* and usually have a fabric doll figure in relief on their reverse sides.

In the week or so following New Year, children in bright kimono can be seen all through the streets batting the hanetsuki pellets back and forth. There is no net; the object of the game is more or less to keep the pellet in the air.

Next time you see such a match on the street, ask to join in. Lots of fun.

Well, these are the typically Japanese sports, though the sports-loving Japanese have adopted most Western games as their own by now. Second to baseball in popularity, perhaps, is golf, in spite of its great expense for the average Japanese. Horse racing is most popular, with the fillies racing clockwise instead of counterclockwise as in the Occident, and with a most curious system of betting, which to date I have been unable to fathom. Tennis is popular, and since the famed romance between Crown Prince Akihito and Michiko Shoda, which began on the tennis court, even more so. There is no American football, but soccer and rugby are played among school teams. Japanese are excellent skiers, skaters, and mountaineers. And, of course, superb swimmers. There is a good deal of boxing—more, now that television is well-established. And for this same reason there now is almost as much of that abysmal fakery known as "pro" wrestling.

Japanese athletes put unbelievably hard work into their careers. It may be that the smaller frames and statures of the Japanese give them an inferiority complex to overcome; at any rate, when a Japanese decides to become proficient at some form of athletics, he literally knocks himself out in training. What's more, on the playing field, he is a most dogged performer. I have seen knocked-out boxers rise, groggy-eyed, before the count of ten and, unable to lift their hands, stand there and let themselves be knocked down again. There is in the Japanese athlete a wonderful never-say-die spirit that is often awesome to behold. Perhaps it has its roots in the samurai tradition. Whatever the origin, it makes Japanese sport a real thrill for the foreign visitor.

chapter seventeen

the theater arts

Second in number only to the inveterate tourists are the inveterate theater-goers. The more diligent of the breed will travel halfway around the world to visit a country, and then spend their stay in darkened theaters vicariously living in the condensed world of the stage before them.

But, as it happens, Japan's theater reflects much of the true nature of the country. The Japanese are superb at make-believe. Their *Kabuki* theater is breathtaking; their even more traditional and ancient *Noh* plays are rich in interest, and their famed *Bun-*

raku puppet shows are an art in themselves. Even the Japanese cinema—as we shall presently see—affords an insight into this island world.

kabuki   Let us begin with Kabuki, justly the most famous of Japan's theater arts. Kabuki takes place on a stage one hundred feet wide, on which dragons snort, houses collapse before your eyes, and, quite as often, ghostly ectoplasm dances. There is magnificent stagecraft and a judicious wedding of the drama and the dance. It is unlike any theater you will see anywhere else in the world and in spite of the language barrier it is seldom boring.

Kabuki is often spoken of as "the traditional theater of Japan," but actually it's more popular than a relic of mere historical interest might be. In many ways it resembles the Western world's Shakespearean theater. Roughly, it's about as old as Shakespeare. Like the bard's plays, Kabuki dramas were originally written and produced for rather ordinary people. The subject matter ranges from broad comedy to deep tragedy and many of the plays have an historical setting. They are also, like Shakespearean drama, full of certain conventions: the speeches are often poetry and they are declaimed in a highly stylized fashion instead of delivered with the almost too intimate realism we usually see in, say, motion picture acting today. Kabuki's traditionally favorite plays are performed year after year, but new ones also appear each season. This has led to an outgrowth of Kabuki, a more realistic modern theater which is called Shimpa. It's my personal feeling that Shimpa hasn't nearly the style and elegance of Kabuki, and, in attempting to compromise between the old and the new, fails as an art form. Either Kabuki itself—or a frankly modern, Western-style play—seems to be more successful.

But let's get an idea of what we'll see if we attend the Kabuki theater. The word *Kabuki,* I'm told, comes from the verb *kabuku,* which means to incline or deviate—to get away from the orthodox method of doing something. Centuries ago there was a shrine in Japan called Izumo, and occasionally they would put on what we would call today a fund-raising campaign. To make money they'd stage certain revue-like entertainments, at first called *Kabuki,* because they weren't quite like the usual plays of the time. From this: *Kabuki,* whose written characters, by themselves, mean song-dance technique.

Kabuki usually employs its own form of the Japanese language, differing from the modern tongue perhaps as Shakespearean English differs from our own. Fortunately, the stories are usually easy to follow even if you don't know Japanese. You will ordinarily find synopses of the plots printed in English in your programs. Naturally, in the plays, there will be long passages of pure conversation, and this may bore you a little, but on the whole your eye will be intrigued by movement, color, and design from beginning to end.

Kabuki shows are long. The theater usually opens at 11:00 a.m. and continues to 9:00 p.m. The performance will be in two parts, morning and evening, and you can buy tickets for either or both. Sometimes one long play will be given; sometimes several shorter plays. Now and then mere acts or other fragments from favorite plays will be presented. Often there will be a special dancing number of some kind interspersed between acts or plays. In either morning or evening session there will be a number of intermissions during which you can get various snacks in the stalls and restaurants that are part of the theater itself.

Every major city in Japan has one or more Kabuki theaters. There is seldom any stage presentation in the United States quite as spectacular as Kabuki. For one thing the United States is big, physically, and the center of the American stage is New York. Obviously, everyone in the country can't get to New York to patronize the theater. Thus, not so many attend live theater as in Japan. Kabuki—nearly always sold out—is both popular and profitable; the producers have more money to spend on their sets and costumes. Their expenses are not so high. In the United States an electrician or stagehand belongs to a tight union and often makes more per week than some of the actors. As for sets, most of the Kabuki plays come from a standard repertoire and thus most of the items don't have to be built or procured anew.

When you come to Kabuki and take your seat you will see, first, a huge silk curtain drawn across a tremendous stage. This curtain usually has broad vertical stripes. It is drawn open rather than raised. As the drama begins you will hear a clacking of resonant sticks, at first slowly, and then in gradually increasing tempo. The mood music will be supplied by a small group of men on a platform at one side of the stage, or perhaps hidden there by a screen of some sort. Three singers and three samisen players make up a typical group. They wear ancient costumes. During the play one or more singers will often act as narrator, weaving chanted comment into the action and dialogue.

During the play you may see such effects as waterfalls or full-scale storms with lightning and thunder. Sets flip over or change by means of a huge, revolving stage. A good play usually has a few dances worked into it, and everyone looks forward to the sword fights which, instead of being shown realistically, are treated rather as dances in themselves.

The real fans always know what's coming next, and this no more spoils their enjoyment than previous knowledge spoils *Hamlet* or *Rigoletto*. Veteran Kabuki-goers also know what to shout and when to shout it. There are certain favorite moments in all of the plays; certain poses or attitudes the audience expects and waits for. When an actor does a particularly good job someone in the audience is sure to call out: *"Matte imashita!"*—"That's what we've been waiting for!" Or they may shout the actor's name. This will be his special Kabuki name which he gets according to a complicated formula too involved to explain here. Roughly speaking, his appellation is based on the name of a famous actor of the past, and a number is added to show where he stands in line of succession. Often it is the number alone that is shouted out in appreciation.

In Kabuki, applause comes only at certain places. It may be just before the curtain is opened, to show that you've been waiting eagerly. You can applaud a difficult or effective pose. Japanese audiences never applaud after the play is ended and Kabuki actors never take curtain calls. They're applauded sometimes on the long runway that comes down from the back of the house to the stage— just as in an Occidental burlesque theater. This runway is called the *hanamichi,* or flower way.

Onstage, men in black costumes often scoot out to change the scenery, or to take away an actor's overgarments when he discards them. Their black costumes mean that you can't see them.

As for the actors themselves, they spend long apprenticeships and then lifetimes at their craft. Some are still active in their seventies, and then play women's or younger men's parts. Children begin by playing children. All actors are male, by the way, and the illusion of femininity the *onnagata,* or female impersonators manage to create is one of the remarkable things about Kabuki. On close scrutiny these spurious females are seldom beautiful. But with their clear falsetto voices and womanish movements they soon have you believing their characterizations, whether they are playing old crones or ingenues. A Kabuki fan will tell you that an onnagata, as a result of long study, knows more about woman than woman herself. They are not, as you will often hear, necessarily homosexual; many have large families.

You buy your tickets, enter the theater, and find your seats in

Kabuki much as you do in any theater; there is no strangeness of approach to make you feel awkward should you decide to attend. The plays, with their recurring themes of feudal and filial obligation, of murder, mayhem, ghosts, and suicide, are a most interesting reflection of Japanese ways of thought. Humor in Kabuki usually follows the pattern of the stuffed shirt getting pricked and exploding, which is a satisfactory sort of laughter for almost anyone.

Famed American playwrights who visit Japan head for the Kabuki theater swiftly. You will find it rewarding to do the same.

noh drama   You have to be something of a student of Japanalia to get anything out of Noh. Noh is Japan's most traditional, aristocratic, and highly stylized form of theater. It is even closer to the dance than is Kabuki. Usually each section of Noh starts with a dialogue which explains the action, and then the dancing or movement follows, carrying out the action. There is a commentary by a chanting chorus of six or eight narrators, and music by flutes and drums. The actors wear masks and move in prescribed, tiny steps on a stage much smaller than the Kabuki platform—usually about eighteen feet square.

The language of Noh is even more classical than that of Kabuki, and for this reason the general public in Japan neither understands nor appreciates the form. But to the foreigner Noh presents a kind of weird beauty which is certainly worth experiencing at least once.

The masks used in Noh are popular as souvenirs for foreigners. They represent heroes and villains, certain animals, legendary gods, and historical characters. They're often exquisitely made and serve as fine, decorative wall hangings. You can find them in shops nearly everywhere, even in department stores.

takarazuka and kokusai

Kabuki is the all-male theater in Japan, but it has its distaff counterpart. This is found in the all-girl revues put on in Japan's large cities, particularly in Tokyo. In the capital there are three houses devoted to these spectacular modern variety shows. and, as in Kabuki, the stage presentations are apt to be far and away more elaborate than anything found in New York, London, or Paris.

The most famous of these revue troupes is the Takarazuka Opera Company, which now has units both in Tokyo and in its original home near Osaka. Its girls have long been considerd the most beautiful in Japan. The whole thing started back in 1912 when a man named Kobayashi organized a revue in a small resort town near Osaka for a rather oblique reason. It seemed he owned a railroad from Osaka to the resort town, whose name was Takarazuka, (pronounced Tah-kah-rahz'-kah), and in order to get customers to ride his trains he decided to put on a show.

Kobayashi broke with tradition. Until then men had played all the parts in the Japanese theater. He reversed the procedure —nothing but women on his stage. His idea was an immediate success, and by 1940 the company controlled five hundred theaters and you could find more than six hundred girls singing, dancing, and acting in one special traveling show.

Takarazuka, then, was the original all-girl lavish revue; it has been followed by Kokusai, a Tokyo company, and paralleled to a degree by Tokyo's Nichigeki Theater, which is basically dedicated to what are called strip shows, but which manages, nevertheless, to put on elaborate productions, differing from the other two companies by employing a mixed cast of males and females, and by featuring night-club, motion-picture, and television stars in its revues.

In the all-girl companies performers are carefully selected for excellence of face and figure, then, as apprentices, carefully trained in the arts of the stage. Entrance requirements are high; usually only about sixty out of every hundred applicants make the grade. Beginners must be between sixteen and nineteen years of age, and twenty-one years is the limit for girls with previous training.

Most of the instructors have learned their trade in New York or Paris. They teach every style of dancing, from the ancient Japanese court movements to the most aphrodisiac contemporary mambo. At a revue there is always a rapid change of mood and pace. Traditional scenes give way to raucous jazz numbers by means of flipping backdrops and revolving stages; much of the stagecraft is borrowed from Kabuki, and you're likely to find such items as real waterfalls or exploding mountains as part of the scene. The various skits have plots, more or less, but it isn't necessary to know the stories or understand the dialogue. The visual pleasure alone is worth the trip . . . and the precision dances of the chorus line bring back, to those old enough to remember, the famed Rockettes or Ziegfeld Follies girls of a bygone day in America . . . .

chambara   Those who know what *chambara* is will be a little surprised to see it under the heading of Theater Arts. I claim that it's both Theater and Art—perhaps not at a high level, but significant as far as Japan is concerned and therefore worth seeing. Chambara is a type of sword battle that occurs in certain Japanese plays and motion pictures. The movies that use chambara are the Japanese equivalent of the American "'Western' film—or horse opera, if you prefer.

Chambara is like the horse opera in four respects. First, it deals with a romantic period of the country's history. Second, it shows this history as it probably never was. Third, it deals with violence: taut emotions, primitive ideals. Fourth, all chambara movies have pretty much the same plot. ("An adult Western," says a cynical producer friend of mine, "is one where the plot is at least twenty-one years old.")

But there are some positive values and these too resemble the American Western film. No matter how bad a horse opera is, it's pretty hard to destroy the scenery, and chambara has the same advantage. The settings and costumes are often exquisite and since the Japanese people seem to have an inborn talent for the visual, the cinematography is often outstanding.

Like the Western, the chambara movie is made up of ingredients that seldom change. To begin, there's always the samurai code of honor, which we've discussed in a previous chapter. *Hara-kiri* or, preferably, *seppuku* figures largely in these Japanese morality plays. The hero is usually depicted as a pretty noble character. But where our Western hero is tall and slim, the chambara lead is quite often apt to be a bit on the chubby side, and I think it may be that a stout man always seems a little more solid, a little more prosperous to the Japanese. The climax of a Western movie frequently shows a gun duel between the hero and villain, the two of them facing each other in the dusty street of the town, with all other characters either conveniently killed by now or else hiding behind rain barrels in order not to clutter up the action. In chambara, the odds are increased in the villain's favor. The chambara hero, toward the end, faces not one, but twenty or thirty villains at a time. His sword goes snicker-snack and they fall in twos and threes. The sword never seems to touch the victims, but this apparently never bothers chambara fans. And when the victims are struck they are always killed outright, never merely disabled; they never display the kicking and carry-ingon you might expect to accompany death by decapitation or disembowelment.

Chambara, the name of this genre, is an onomatopoetic word. The agitated music that accompanies the action in these films goes: *chan-chan barra-barra*; *chan-barra-chan!*—hence, *chambara.* Such films are also known, sometimes, as *ken-geki,* or "sword play."

To introduce you to this wonderful art form I have concocted a synthetic chambara story, which I now present to you on a wide screen and in full color:

"Enjoy Japan" Presents:

the sad-sack samurai

As our tale opens two great families of Japan are feuding with each other. This is hardly surprising, since this is feudal Japan. But so far all they've been doing is going around making feudal gestures.

We pick up our hero as he rides toward a secret rendezvous at night, is waylaid by fifty or sixty soldiers of the opposite clan, cuts them all down, and proceeds on to the old ruined temple where he has a date with his girl friend.

Our hero's name is Shin-no-suke. He's in love with the daughter of the chief of the other clan, and her name is Princess Chiyo. As they meet in the moonlight, she says to him:

CHIYO: 戦が終れば結ばれませう. ("If you samurai would stop horsing around and killing each other, we could get married.")

So Shin-no-suke decides to put an end to the feud once and for all. And the only way to do that is to kill the man behind it all, the chief adviser to his sweetheart's clan, a man we shall call Hata. All of this comes out in the dialogue as Shin-no-suke and

Chiyo pant over each other in the moonlight. It makes the love talk a little unnatural, but, hell's bells, you've got to get this plot information in *some* way. Now we—

DISSOLVE TO: *Exterior. The castle moat. Night.*

In the dead of night Shin-no-suke swims the moat, climbs the walls, and makes his way past the sentries, managing to kill a few dozen who try to stop him. But when he reaches the inner citadel of the castle, he finds that Hata, the wicked chief adviser, has been expecting him all along.

You see, Hata had his favorite geisha, disguised as a scullery maid and working in Shin-no-suke's household all the time, overhear our hero's plans. I don't know exactly how to work this information in without slowing up the action at this point— maybe we should have started the whole story a ways back. Oh, well, we'll let the director worry about this detail.

Anyway, it's a trap. As Shin-no-suke enters the inner courtyard, he finds fifty of Hata's samurai waiting for him, swords drawn. There is a tremendous battle. Shin-no-suke cuts down the opposing samurai in convenient groups and before long has disposed of all of them, including the wicked Hata.

Princess Chiyo runs out into the moonlight to greet her lover.

CHIYO: 進之介様, これで私共も一緒になれませう. ("Now we can Lohengrin it, Daddy.")

But then Princess Chiyo suddenly looks at all the dead men scattered like chaff upon the ground, and as suddenly takes a closer look at one of the bodies.

A terrible mistake has been made! Her father—the head of the clan—thought he'd get in a little sport, and so had disguised himself as an ordinary samurai and joined the attack upon our hero. Now he lies dead with the rest. (No blood, no brains spattered on the paving—just dead.)

CHIYO: (Tearfully) こうなっては私共は一緒になる事は出来ません. ("I reckon this spoils the wedding plans, partner.")

CLOSE UP OF CHIYO. She gnashes her teeth to show emotion.

CLOSE UP OF SHIN-NO-SUKE. He gnashes on a bagel.

DISSOLVE TO:

EXTERIOR. A SHRINE. DAY.

Shin-no-suke is kneeling before the shrine, gripping his short suicide sword in a fresh piece of Kleenex. His friend (I'm sorry—I forgot to mention his friend before, but I guess the director will have sense enough to work him in somewhere earlier) stands by with another sword to lop off Shin-no-suke's head after the fatal cut is made.

Suddenly Princess Chiyo, more or less breathless, rushes upon the scene.

CHIYO: 切腹はお待ちあそばせ進之介様. ("Knock it off, fellas—hold everything!")

It seems that the chief of her clan, the old man her lover killed, wasn't her father after all! He was an imposter all the time. Her father, the real head of the clan, is selling noodles from a cart, waiting for the right moment to avenge himself. Now the two lovers can get married and unite the two clans for a peaceful, happy future.

You think this is the end? Better go out and get another box of popcorn.

CLOSE UP OF CHIYO. Glycerine drops roll down her cheeks. She bites a lock of her hair. CUT TO:

FULL SHOT. Our hero, Shin-no-suke walks toward the top of a hill, waving, then disappears over its crest. He has changed his mind about getting married. He now realizes that it's his duty to fight for the new combined clan and, as a wandering warrior, he can't be saddled with a wife and the probable brood of squawling brats she'd produce for him.

MUSIC UP and view of Mt. Fuji, majestic against the lonely sky.

FADE OUT, THE END.

I wouldn't be surprised to see a Japanese producer take even this sow's ear of a yarn and turn it into a fine, silk-purse production. It might even win a prize at an international film festival. But it'd still be chambara.

chapter eighteen

the womanly arts—
kimono and flowers

the kimono You would think that basically it's nothing but a long robe with a sash around the middle, and you wouldn't suppose there was anything particularly difficult either in making or wearing the kimono. But these are two things virtually no foreigners and, for that matter, by no means the majority of Japanese do well. When a well-made kimono is worn well, you notice it. And in this case the kimono becomes one of the loveliest costumes in the world, flattering to just about any female figure.

Except for small details, the style of the kimono hasn't changed for centuries. A young Japanese lady could stroll through the streets today wearing her grandmother's kimono with just a few slight modifications, and no one would raise an eyebrow. Indeed, this happens often enough, for fine kimono are usually handed down through several generations.

Before World War II most Japanese women wore kimono; today perhaps eighty percent wear Western costumes, which are much more practical for living in modern Japan. For one thing, it takes a half hour or so to don a kimono properly—that's minimum. Second, no one can run to catch a train or bus in a kimono. Third, the kimono is not quite so comfortable a garment for all-day wear as you might think. However, the kimono is still worn a great deal on special occasions: at New Year, perhaps; at family celebrations; at the Kabuki theater, and even at the cinema.

The full kimono costume has a great many parts and a lore all its own, but the basic garment is simplicity itself. It is made according to an unvarying pattern from a bolt of cloth 34', 4" long and fourteen inches wide. This is cut into certain strips and oblongs which form the body and sleeves of the garment. Most Japanese housewives are familiar with the pattern, though they usually trust the cutting and sewing of a kimono to an expert seamstress. Many visiting American and European women, intrigued by the exquisite colors and patterns of kimono material, feel they would like to have dresses made from it, but because of the narrowness of the bolt of cloth this is usually fairly difficult. The next best thing, they often find, is to get a kimono outfit of their own.

Usually some adjustments have to be made for the foreign visitor. The standard kimono is made for a woman five to five and a half feet tall. To dress in a kimono properly, a number of undergarments and accessories are needed. You start with two underpieces, a sort of shirtwaist-and-petticoat combination whose parts are called, respectively, *hada-juban* and *koshimaki*. Over this goes another thin undergarment shaped like the kimono itself, and this is the *naga-juban*. These pieces are fastened by a series of waist sashes of silk in various colors. The kimono goes on top, and is pulled together at the waist by an undersash, then folded over this sash so that the length is exactly right. Exactly right means that the bottom hem should touch the instep, but not the floor.

The *obi,* or outer sash, is almost a garment in itself. It's usually about four and a half yards long and a foot or more wide. Ordinarily it's made of silk (though cheaper ones are rayon) and it's a very heavy silk indeed. In a sense it acts like an outer corset. A fine obi can cost as much as a thousand dollars, but a very good one can be bought for twenty. Over the obi there's a decorated cord that holds it in place. The bow of the obi, worn in back, is the key to its character. Tying this bow properly is most difficult, even with the various bustle effects that fit under the knot to make it stand upright. You can buy obi ready-tied, of course, but with these, as with men's bow ties, the effect is never quite right. There are also, in these modern times, obi fastened with hooks and zippers. Nothing, however, looks quite so graceful as the old-fashioned kimono properly draped, with the obi correctly tied by hand.

The style of the bow-knot is a language all its own, for the married woman's obi differs from the geisha's, the young maiden's from the divorcee's. If, as a foreigner, you buy a kimono, it's best to consult a Japanese woman for the proper style of bow to fit you and your station in life.

Be prepared to spend a good sum if you want to own a complete kimono outfit. A good one may run from seventy to a hundred dollars. You can do it for less with inferior material, but this is not advisable.

As kimono accessories you'll want *tabi*—little split-toed socks, usually white—and *zori,* or sandals. There are also special styles of handbags and purses to go with the kimono. And in cold weather either velvet or woolen shawls or fur neckpieces may be worn.

In warmer seasons a much simpler and less costly variation of kimono style is the *yukata.* This is a cotton garment usually printed with most attractive designs and worn with a lighter and less complicated obi. It may even be held together by a simple narrow sash called a *datemaki,* though this is considered rather informal.

The kimono also calls for a short coat known as a *haori.* This is worn on the street and may be removed indoors if you wish. In general, young people wear bright colors, older people quieter hues. Kimono and haori will often bear little printed circular marks, each perhaps the size of a silver dollar, whose designs show the wearer's family crest. Men's kimono usually come in black, gray, or brown.

Although modern dress is worn for practically all purposes in Japan, it seems, at this writing, at least, that the kimono will be around the Ancient Isles of Yamato for a long time to come.

flower arrangement
In the Western world a bunch of flowers is grabbed by the throat and shoved into a vase any old way. In Japan, it's much different. And Japanese flower arranging is one of the cheapest and most rewarding hobbies you can follow in Japan, then take home with you afterward when you return to your own part of the world.

There are flower shops in every neighborhood and in them flowers are most reasonable. Once, when I had been in Japan only a short time, I stopped in such a shop to get a corsage for a beautiful young lady I was taking to the theater. The orchids were so cheap that I bought five of them. (This is the masculine mind at work.) The young lady hesitated to pin them on and finally, in a most apologetic fashion, said what amounted to: "Really—too much!" She was right. We threw four orchids away without a qualm.

Simplicity is the keynote of Japanese flower arranging—that and the illusion that the flowers grow out of the vase rather than just sitting there waiting to die. Flower arrangement has been practiced in Japan for centuries and is generally supposed to have originated with an ancient noble who wanted his floral offerings to Buddha to have what a modern ad man would call visual appeal. Through the years it has developed into a formal and at times a complicated art, and today there are a number of schools of flower arranging—sects, if you will—each with its own fiercely held theories and conventions.

The principles of arrangement, however, are the same for all schools. There are always three main parts of any finished composition: *shin,* the first stem; *soe,* the second, and *hikae,* the third. Added to these are the subordinate branches and foofooraw called *jushi*. There is a notation for flower arrangements, a kind of floral choreography, and in it the elements we have just mentioned are symbolized by a circle, square, triangle, and large T.

Vases and receptacles are most important, and are always selected to fit the flowers and branches used. Most often they are flat and shallow, though any shape may be found. Accessories include small metal plates with spikes arranged as in a fakir's bed; the stems are thrust upon these and thus held upright. Often the cut stems are treated with a special solution and held for a moment in a flame to close the pores and keep them fresh longer.

The hobbyist will also find himself with a collection of special scissors and knives for flower arranging.

Instruction in flower arranging is most reasonable in Japan. After a little inquiry it's quite easy to find a school or engage a private teacher to come to your dwelling. If you have a little aptitude and stick at it long enough, you will be awarded various diplomas to show your degree of attainment. The highest of these is held, currently, by an Australian resident who is not a woman, but a man. Flower arranging is by no means exclusively a feminine wile.

The two main schools might be called "natural" and "formal" schools. The first tries to use nature itself as a model; the second aims at a classical ideal. Both of these schools are split into a number of sects. The best known to foreigners, perhaps, is the *Sogetsu* style, which parallels the approach of modern painting in the graphic arts. Sogetsu makes arrangements not only of flowers, but of wire, straw, plastic, driftwood, and—one of these days, no doubt —the kitchen sink.

One thing's certain. After an introduction to Japanese flower arrangement you'll never again thrust a bunch of posies willy-nilly into a milk bottle without wincing.

chapter nineteen

the japanese language—or why you should study spanish

When you step from the plane or boat and onto Japanese soil you are sure to encounter a trinket or souvenir shop almost before you've run the gantlets of customs and immigration. There, among other items, you're bound to find several language and phrase books for sale, all of them optimistic titles like: *Japanese Overnight* or *Two Minutes a Day to Mastery of the Nippon Tongue.*

Don't you believe it.

You can, however, in quite a short time, pick up enough elementary Japanese to treble the enjoyment of your stay in the islands. Already a number of Japanese words have become part of the daily vocabulary of Americans serving with their military forces over here. Unfortunately some of these have become so Anglicized by now that they're no longer recognizable as Japanese and are useful only in bars or cabarets adjoining military bases.

There are also English words now in regular use by the Japanese, and many of these have long ago lost their English flavor. But this exchange is a beginning.

Now, in this short chapter it would be foolish to make an attempt to teach any of the language. But what I would like to acquaint you with is the character and general form of Japanese so that you won't start out *thinking* in English, and trying to substitute your newly learned Japanese words for their English counterparts. This is the key to the matter; you must think in a slightly different way. The sound of Japanese must also be learned anew. If your foreign accent and intonation are too strong, you will be unintelligible. Mark Twain understood this matter well. Once, when his wife decided to cure him of swearing, she stood before him and in her ladylike voice reeled off all of his favorite cusswords, hoping the shock would do something to him. He looked up at her and laughed. "You know the words, my dear," he said, "But you don't know the tune!"

There is a tune to English, a tune to Japanese. The important thing to learn first is the *notation* of the Japanese tune. And this is simply the Japanese way of writing. But I don't mean the Chinese characters that form the bulk of any Japanese written text. I mean the special auxiliary set of characters—there are only fifty-one sounds—the Japanese themselves invented to represent the phonics of their language.

This auxiliary writing is called *kana,* and there are two styles: *kata-kana* and *hira-gana.* The two styles resemble each other as perhaps our print and handwriting do, though they serve slightly different purposes. Kata-kana, the stiffer and more angular of the two, is used for all foreign words adopted into the Japanese language, and it's also popular for signs, trademarks, and advertisements because of its simplicity. Hira-gana is used mainly where there is no Chinese character to represent the word or sound desired. We'll not attempt to reproduce the two syllabaries here, for there are plenty of good books from which you can learn them. But we will discuss their nature, which is the real basis of Japanese word structure and pronunciation.

Originally *all* Japanese was written with characters borrowed from the Chinese. Even today Japanese can read most Chinese writing, though they pronounce the words differently. Horse, for example, in most Chinese dialects, is "ma." In Japanese you say "uma." But in both languages it is written with the same character.

Now, Chinese has a rather simpler structure than Japanese and doesn't make nearly so much use of the various small words of the kind we call prepositions. The Japanese, however, have ways of saying "to, from, in, on, during, within," and so on. Instead of using *pre*-positions—words stuck in front of the main word— they use *post*-positions, or, more accurately, particles. These are nothing more than short syllables tacked on to the words they pertain to. We say "in Tokyo"; Japanese say "Tokyo-in." They also attach other little syllables to their words to show if they're subjects, objects, or other parts of a sentence. All this is grammar, and, according to the best recent thinking on learning languages, shouldn't be worried about. But it's necessary to use these terms for just a moment to describe the nature of Japanese.

Japanese has also adopted a great many foreign words, from English, Portuguese, Dutch, and other languages. And, since the time when only Chinese writing was used, a great many new Japanese words (for which there are no Chinese characters) have been invented. It was clear quite early in the game that Chinese writing alone wouldn't express Japanese very efficiently. And so the auxiliary writing, or kana was developed.

Chinese characters stand for whole words. Kana characters stand for syllables or sounds. There are fifty-one of these phonemes.

This makes Japanese a language not very rich in sound: English, for example, has eleven vowel sounds alone. The English vowel "o" can be pronounced as in "hole," "got," "money," "long," "port," and so on. In Japanese "o" is *always* pronounced the same way "ō" as in "hole." Always. And the other four vowels have their, single, consistent pronunciation each. In other words, there are only five vowel sounds in Japanese. They are "a" as in father; "e" as in the Spanish peso; "ee" as in weed; "oo" as in brood; and "o" as in rope.

You will notice that I write these sounds phonetically, and not as the vowel letters: a, e, i, u, o. This is an important concept. You must grasp this right away, even if you're only going to look into the Japanese language superficially. *The Japanese do not spell.* Not as we spell, at any rate. Our way of writing is foreign and unnatural to them, although nearly all Japanese study it and call it *romaji* because it is based on Roman characters. But when a Japanese thinks, for example, of the word Coca Cola, he does not see the spelling of it in his mind. He thinks merely of four characters of the kana which stand, respectively, for the order of sounds: "Koh-kah Koh-rah."

(Note the last syllable—"rah." Our "l" sound is difficult for the Japanese and they tend to substitute a kind of "r" sound for it. By the same token this Japanese "r" sound is really most difficult for *us* to reproduce correctly. A Japanese friend of mine has been speaking good English for twenty years but to this day cannot hear the difference between glass and grass.)

And so, ideally, if you want to learn spoken Japanese, you should never attempt to read or write a Japanese word in romaji —our Western way of writing. If you must have a notation system it will be well to learn the kana, which is fairly simple and doesn't take long to memorize. Signs written in kana are all over the landscape in Japan and you can get plenty of practice just walking or riding through any populated area. In this way you'll never be tempted to visualize a Japanese word as it is spelled in English and give it an English pronunciation or intonation.

This advice, by the way, works in reverse for Japanese studying English. They tend to note their English words in kana and, visualizing these syllables, then speaking the English, they often give it a positively weird form. It once took me days to discover that a Japanese friend of mine, asking if I was familiar with "Donarra Doc," meant "Donald Duck." And communication can drop to a very low level when a Japanese refers to "boku-sheeng" and merely means "boxing."

But back to the kana. All the syllables of kana—which is to say all the basic sounds of Japanese—*end in vowels*. There is only one exception, and that is a pure "n" sound, which is tacked on to other syllables when necessary. And this succession of vowelly syllables gives Japanese its somewhat liquid character . . . just as the many consonant-ending syllables impart to English a crisp, staccato sound.

The kana table starts off with a, i, u, e, o. These are all pronounced in something close to the Italian manner: ah, ee, oo, eh, oh. Next come other syllables: *ka, ki, ku, ke, ko; sa, shi, su, se, so,* et cetera. Fifty-one altogether . . . and then a few diphthongs, or combinations of the basic sounds, and a small table of what are called turbid sounds, which mean nothing more than turning *ka, ki, ku, ke, ko,* for example, into *ga, gi, gu, ge, go*. There are a few slight variations along the way. Japanese do not find it easy to say "si" and say "shi" instead. But basically a mere perusal of this table will do much to give you the *feeling* of the Japanese language.

There is one point that may confuse you sometime. There have been several systems of romaji and you may run into the same words spelled according to one of the older systems. In downtown Tokyo there is a hotel called "Daichi" or "First," but a plaque at the entrance says "Daiti Hotel." In both cases it is the same word merely spelled according to a different method of romaji.

As for intonation, Japanese is rather like French. The Japanese, in fact, find French one of the easiest foreign languages for them to learn. In English we usually stress one syllable of a word and stress it by force, by hitting it harder, as it were. We say "syllable" and punch that "syl." In Japanese, the stress is not one of force, but rather of pitch. To accent a syllable in Japanese you raise the tone of your voice just slightly. It's rather a subtle thing, but you'll catch on to it after a few hearings. For a good example ask a Japanese friend to say for you, in Japanese: "How much does it cost?" This is *ikura des'ka?* Most English-speaking persons, reading this, would tend to say: "ee-koo'-rah des'-kah?" hitting that second syllable, "koo," with an accent of force. Actually, the accent—of pitch, not force—is on the first syllable of *ikura.* This can't be written satisfactorily, so you will simply have to get someone to demonstrate it for you in sound.

While we're on the subject of kana we might mention in passing that some syllables of Japanese are barely voiced, so that the vowel in each becomes almost silent. We have just given you the word "des'ka?"—meaning "is it?" The strict spelling of this in romaji is *desuka.* In Japanese kana it consists of three syllables, *de, su,* and *ka.* But in that second syllable—su—the "u" or "oo" sound is scarcely voiced. And so it sounds much more like "des'-ka." This can happen to both "u" and "i" sounds in Japanese. It happens in sukiyaki, which we discussed in the chapter on food. The pronunciation is more like "s'kiyaki." It happens in the word for "do," which is *shite,* and which consists of two kana syllables: *shi* and *te.* But when you say both together it comes out rather like a German with a particularly fat lip asking you to stay. "Shtay" is a close phonetic representation.

Then, alas, we have long and short vowels in Japanese. And the length of the vowel can often make quite a difference. *Oba-san* means "aunt" or "ma'am" . . . *obā-san* means "grand-mother." You can get into trouble calling a nice looking matron of thirty-five or so a grandmother. The vowels a, i, u, and o may be either short or long. Better have a Japanese friend pronounce them for you to show you the difference.

There are a few other characteristics of the Japanese language you ought to know, not so much to help you learn Japanese as to further your understanding of Japanese people trying to speak English. There is no such thing as "the" or "a" in Japanese. Japanese say simply: "Book is on table." There are no plurals. The sentence just quoted could mean one book on one table, or six books on six tables. You're supposed to get the idea from the general context of the surrounding conversation. And, if we may be grammar-conscious for a moment, Japanese transitive verbs do not necessarily demand a direct object. We always say: "Put it on the table!" Japanese say: "Put on table" . . . or, even more likely, "Put!" They have a way of carrying this over into English when they speak it.

Admittedly English is a most inconsistent language. In teaching it to Japanese I have been at a loss to explain why we say; "Go upstairs" . . . "go *to* school" . . . and "go *to the* store." Oh, I suppose you could wade into a morass of grammar and say: "Well, in the first instance, the word 'upstairs' has the function of an adverb, and in the second instance . . ." but all this seems hardly worth the trouble. Best to be a tyrant about it. Best to say: "That's the way it is—say it that way, and don't ask why."

However, speaking to Japanese in a kind of pidgin baby talk

hardly improves their understanding. Nor does shouting increase the communication level. You'll find it hard, though, to resist these two devices. Especially that of pidgin. I often wonder if instinctively we don't feel that pidgin, with its greater economy, is preferable. And secretly wish we spoke it ourselves.

chapter twenty

the japanese character

In the first two chapters of this book we tried to answer the two questions most frequently asked about the Japanese by visitors who come to their country. There is another and perhaps much more important question that Americans and Europeans ask about the Japanese, but usually only among themselves. It has to do with the apparent paradox of the Japanese character. The question comes in several variations, but it generally has the following pattern:

"How could such charming people turn into such monsters in World War II?"

People who had visited Japan before the big war were appalled at the atrocity reports. People who visited Japan after the big war simply could not believe that the Japanese they saw, and were charmed by, were of the same nation that tortured and beheaded prisoners, raped nurses, and bayoneted nuns. Some, who haven't been able to get below the surface, still can't believe it.

The key to it all is that the Japanese have two standards of behavior. But before you decide that this is peculiar it is well to remember that most peoples have. Americans make a fetish of being outwardly cynical and "manly" and inside are a most sentimental and sometimes immature people. British like to appear cold and imperturbable—anyone who really knows the British knows they are not. And so it is that the Japanese display exquisite manners and consideration for others *within their smaller group,* such as the family, the immediate circle of friends, the school, the company, the village. But when a Japanese finds himself in a different group, or in a vast public group, he is under no such compulsion. And it is here that he is able to discharge much of the rage repressed within him by the necessity to curb his feelings most of the time. Nor is any onus attached to this discharge. It is well understood by his fellow Japanese; it is sympathized with. There is even a Japanese proverb to illustrate, explain, and condone it.

Tabi no haji wa kakisute.

"Throw away your shame in whatever place you visit."

Leave your home town and go to one of the fabulous shore resorts. Get roaring drunk. Stagger through the streets shouting obscenities at the top of your lungs in the dark of morning. Bed yourself with Satan's own sister. It's quite all right—a man's a man for all that and that—but just see that you don't behave that way at home.

But there is another saying which, at first glance, seems to contradict the first. *Go ni itte wa, go ni shitagae*—"Obey the customs of the place where you are," or, "When in Rome do as the Romans do." Except—not quite. This admonition applies when you're staying a while and have already become part of the strange place; when, in other words, you have *joined the new group*.

Of course you may now reasonably ask why the Japanese should be filled with all this repressed rage that explodes when the restrictions of group behavior are lifted. Like so much in the Japanese personality, this goes back to the physical nature of the islands in which they live. Japan is crowded. Most often too many people live in one house, and there are far too many houses in a block. There is little room to shout, little room to swing one's elbows, little room to express one's self with any vigor at all. Once I lived in the American West and an old cowboy I met had a fine description of circumstances like these. I asked him how he'd liked the eastern United States and he allowed as how it was all right except "there wasn't room to cuss a cat in." This is certainly true of Japan.

And so the Japanese move softly. They keep their elbows in. They have long lists of prescribed statements and responses designed to soothe ruffled feelings. There is a complex pattern of obligations and social behavior *within the small group*. And even their artistic expression is turned inward rather than outward. The Japanese do not have picture windows; they have exquisite, small, fenced-in gardens. They do not tend to paint sweeping landscapes—rather, a deft bamboo leaf, or a sprig of pine.

Living in crowded conditions can also make one most aware

of the general dangers of life and of the inescapable fact that who-ever gains something for himself most generally takes it away from others. Therefore, the Japanese feels most secure when he is liked—when he is loved, if you will. This may sound like a curious statement, but I'm convinced it's true. Above all things the Japanese wants you to love him, and only when he thinks that you do can he feel quite safe. What is more, he will return that love or regard a hundredfold.

There are some Japanese who, like Americans or Europeans, find it unbearable that they need love so desperately. Then they will deny love: they will attempt to prove to themselves and everyone else that they can walk alone. But this is hardly para-doxical—it is elementary psychology.

Hardly anyone will deny that there is, for Caucasians, and as a matter of fact, for other Asians, an often indefinable "different-ness" about the Japanese. The Japanese themselves admit this, and often, alas, rather revel in it. Yet modern Japanese are fast losing this "differentness" and doing so quite willingly. More and more, as their economy climbs, they are having the opportunity to travel. More and more, thinking Japanese are saying that travel is the thing Japanese need most—a good, hard look at the rest of the world. There is some fear that if Japan becomes too Westernized it will lose its peculiar traditional charm, but those who see the matter in enough depth know that this is hardly true.

Our own Western civilization is based on a Judeo-Christian ethic. Japanese civilization is based on a kind of practical family or group morality. In the family concept the presence of a leader or "father" to make all the decisions as they come up, one by one, is quite necessary. In the nation he is the emperor; in the company, the boss; in the school, the teacher. But take him away and leave a Japanese on his own, and he, the Japanese, is rather at a loss to make moral decisions.

Look at a typical Japanese room some time. There is nearly always a single overhead electric bulb. If this bulb goes out, everyone in the room is in the dark. In most Occidental rooms there are several lamps scattered around so that each occupant has his own light. Judeo-Christian morality may be compared to these individual lights which are there to give guidance in all situations. The Occidental therefore carries his own moral light around with him—we sometimes speak of it as his conscience. For the Japanese there is only one conscience per group. When a Japanese leaves the group he is morally in the dark.

Now, it seems to me that there is something to be gained from both concepts. The Japanese ethic leads to a tremendous sense of group cooperation and a real tolerance and forbearance that would put many a Christian to shame. Japanese turn the other cheek and forgive most easily. On the other hand the Western Judeo-Christian ethic leads to a great deal of individual moral strength which is quite adaptable to changing circumstances. A synthesis of the two should combine the best of each. Today Japan plays host to more foreign visitors than ever before. Host and guest adopt each other's ways, not always choosing the best but, at least, exchanging.

The Japanese understand us better every day, and themselves become more comprehensible. The world shrinks. We all become brothers whether we want to or not. Soon there will be no more places strange enough for us to throw away our shame.

I owe a debt to the Japanese. In learning to love them and their country I have better learned to love mankind.

Nippon wo tanoshinde kudasai. Enjoy Japan.